Truth and Fiction in *The Da Vinci Code*

Truth and Fiction in *The Da Vinci Code*

A Historian Reveals What We Really Know about Jesus, Mary Magdalene, and Constantine

BART D. EHRMAN

OXFORD
UNIVERSITY PRESS

OXFORD
UNIVERSITY PRESS

Oxford University Press, Inc., publishes works that
further Oxford University's objective of excellence
in research, scholarship, and education.

Oxford   New York
Auckland   Cape Town   Dar es Salaam   Hong Kong   Karachi
Kuala Lumpur   Madrid   Melbourne   Mexico City   Nairobi
New Delhi   Shanghai   Taipei   Toronto

With offices in
Argentina   Austria   Brazil   Chile   Czech Republic   France   Greece
Guatemala   Hungary   Italy   Japan   Poland   Portugal   Singapore
South Korea   Switzerland   Thailand   Turkey   Ukraine   Vietnam

First published by Oxford University Press, Inc., 2004
198 Madison Avenue, New York, New York 10016
www.oup.com

First issued as an Oxford University Press paperback, 2006
ISBN-13: 978-0-19-530713-9
ISBN-10: 0-19-530713-5

Oxford is a registered trademark of Oxford University Press

The Library of Congress has cataloged the cloth edition as follows:
Ehrman, Bart D.
Truth and fiction in The Da Vinci Code : a historian reveals what we
really know about Jesus, Mary Magdalene, and Constantine /
by Bart D. Ehrman.
p. cm. Includes index.
ISBN-13: 978-0-19-518140-1   ISBN-10: 0-19-518140-9
1. Brown, Dan, 1964- Da Vinci code.
2. Constantine I, Emperor of Rome, d. 337—In literature.
3. Constantine I, Emperor of Rome, d. 337—Religion.
4. Mary Magdalene, Saint—In literature.
5. Christian saints in literature.
6. Jesus Christ—In literature.
7. Christianity and literature.
8. Christianity in literature.
I. Title.
PS3552.R685434D3335 2004
813'.54—dc22 2004056805

Credits for illustrations. Fig. 1: Vanni/ Art Resource, NY;
Fig. 2a (caves): Bart Ehrman; Fig. 2b (scrolls): Israel Museum, Jerusalem;
Figs. 3 and 4: Institute for Antiquity and Christianity, Claremont, CA;
Fig. 5: British Library, London; Fig. 6: Rylands Library, University of Manchester;
Fig. 7: André Held; Fig. 8: Scala/ Art Resource, NY.

1 3 5 7 9 8 6 4 2
Printed in the United States of America

To Robert Miller, friend and editor extraordinaire

Contents

Part 2: Jesus and Mary Magdalene

Acknowledgments

I would like to thank two people for helping me write this book. The first is my friend and editor at Oxford University Press, Robert Miller, who conceived of the idea, convinced me to pursue it, and read the manuscript with a scrupulous eye to detail. The other is my former student, Andrew Jacobs, at the University of California, Riverside, whose careful and extensive comments on an original draft of the book far exceeded anything that friendship or collegiality could have asked.

Acknowledgments

Introduction

The Da Vinci Code by Dan Brown has been an enormous pub-
lishing success, dwarfing all competitors of recent memory. As I
write these words (June 14, 2004), the book has been on the *New
York Times* best-seller list for sixty-three weeks, where it is still
number one. Earlier this year it was selling at an astronomical
rate of 100,000 copies *per week,* according to the February 9,
2004, issue of *Publishers Weekly.* When the paperback version
comes out, we can expect yet another huge avalanche of sales,
topping the many millions of copies of the hardback already in
print.

Like many others, I first heard of *The Da Vinci Code* by word
of mouth. I had just finished a book called *Lost Christianities: The
Battles for Scripture and the Faiths We Never Knew* for Oxford
University Press. This was a book about forms of early Christianity that never "made it," Christian beliefs and practices that
came to be shunned, outlawed, and destroyed by the leaders of
the early church, who were intent on establishing the orthodox
way of understanding the religion. Included in my book were

lengthy discussions of some of the noncanonical and heretical books that came to be proscribed by early church fathers. These were other Gospels, epistles, and apocalypses that had for one Christian group or another served as sacred scripture but which ran afoul of the authorities who eventually made the decisions concerning what to include in the canon of scripture and what to exclude. As a result of their exclusion, these books came to be lost—and most of them have remained lost to this day, with the exception of some few that have turned up here and there, many of them in remarkable archaeological discoveries of the nineteenth and twentieth centuries.

In addition to my book *Lost Christianities* I published a collection of the survivors of these so-called heretical books in a volume called *Lost Scriptures: Books That Did Not Make It into the New Testament* (also published by Oxford University Press). Both volumes were written not for scholars who are already familiar with such matters but for lay people for whom all this is news.

Naturally, when I learned about *The Da Vinci Code* my interest was piqued, for here was a modern work of fiction—a murder mystery, filled with complicated plots and subplots, conspiracies, unveiled truths—that mentioned, and to some extent was even based on, some of these issues from early Christianity, the lost Gospels and their portrayal of Jesus. But according to *The Da Vinci Code*, these lost Gospels do not represent a heretical understanding of Jesus; they rather portray the historical truth about him—in particular that he was married to Mary Magdalene and that they had a child and thus initiated a holy line that still survives to the present day.

I knew that the book itself was fictional, of course, but as I read it (and for me, as for many others, it was a real page-turner) I realized that Dan Brown's characters were actually making *his-*

torical claims about Jesus, Mary, and the Gospels. In other words, the fiction was being built on a historical foundation that the reader was to accept as factual, not fictitious.

But like most historians who have spent their lives studying the ancient sources for Jesus and early Christianity, I immediately began to see problems with the historical claims made in the book. There were numerous mistakes, some of them howlers, which were not only obvious to an expert but also unnecessary to the plot. If the author had simply done a little bit more research, he would have been able to present the historical backdrop of his account accurately, without in any way compromising the story he had to tell. Why didn't he simply get his facts straight?

Since *The Da Vinci Code* was selling great guns already by the time my book *Lost Christianities* appeared, my publicist at Oxford University Press, Tara Kennedy, along with my longtime editor and friend, Robert Miller, suggested that I come up with a list of historical problems with the book, so that they could give these to our marketing people as an item of interest for anyone who might ask. And so I slapped something together rather quickly, based on a simple reading of Dan Brown's novel. Later this quick list got onto the Internet; it eventually came to be published (with my blessing, but without my giving it an editorial once-over) in one of the recent books that has come out dealing with *The Da Vinci Code*, a book edited by Dan Burstein called *Secrets of the Code: The Unauthorized Guide to the Mysteries Behind The Da Vinci Code*. Burstein is a freelance journalist who has put together a very interesting compilation of opinions on *The Da Vinci Code* by experts (and nonexperts) in a range of fields, from the ancient history of the church (my field) to Leonardo da Vinci to secret societies among the Roman Catholics. Included is my simple list of ten historical problems that I isolated for my publisher. Here they are, unchanged from how I first gave them:

Some Factual Errors in *The Da Vinci Code*

1. Jesus' life was decidedly *not* "recorded by thousands of followers across the land." He didn't even have thousands of followers, let alone literate ones (p. 231).

2. It's not true that eighty Gospels "were considered for the New Testament" (p. 231). This makes it sound like there was a contest, entered by mail. . . .

3. It's absolutely not true that Jesus was not considered divine until the Council of Nicea, that before that he was considered merely as "a mortal prophet" (p. 233). The vast majority of Christians by the early fourth century acknowledged him as divine. (Some thought he was so divine he wasn't even human!)

4. Constantine did *not* commission a "new Bible" that omitted references to Jesus' human traits (p. 234). For one thing, he didn't commission a new Bible at all. For another thing, the books that did get included are chock-full of references to his human traits (he gets hungry, tired, angry; he gets upset; he bleeds, he dies . . .).

5. The Dead Sea Scrolls were not "found in the 1950s" (p. 234). It was 1947. And the Nag Hammadi documents do *not* tell the Grail story at all, nor do they emphasize Jesus' human traits. Quite the contrary.

6. "Jewish decorum" in no way forbade "a Jewish man to be unmarried" (p. 245). In fact, most of the community behind the Dead Sea Scrolls were male unmarried celibates.

7. The Dead Sea Scrolls were not among "the earliest Christian records" (p. 245). They are Jewish, with nothing Christian in them.

8. We have no idea about the lineage of Mary Magdalene; nothing connects her with the "house of Benjamin." And even if she were, this wouldn't make her a descendent of David (p. 248).

9. Mary Magdalene was *pregnant* at the crucifixion? That's a good one (p. 255).

10. The Q document is not a surviving source being hid by the Vatican, nor is it a book allegedly written by Jesus himself. It's a hypothetical document that scholars have posited as having been available to Matthew and Luke, principally a collection of the sayings of Jesus. Roman Catholic scholars think the same of it as non-Catholics; there's nothing secretive about it (p. 256).

In addition to providing this simple list, I was interviewed for Dan Burstein's book, as one of the experts in the field.

And there I thought the matter would end.

But Robert Miller, my Oxford editor, became increasingly convinced that the books that have started to appear about *The Da Vinci Code* are all seriously wanting in one way or another. Some, like Burstein's, are compilations made by people who are interested in the subject but not expert in it; others (a greater number, evidently) are written by religious persons who want to "set the record straight" in case some of their co-religionists (evangelical Christians, mainly?) might be misled by some statements made in the book. These kinds of reactions are fine for what they are. But what about a real response by somebody who is actually an expert in the area? Miller convinced me that there was a need for a historian to respond to Dan Brown's book.

The reasons for my responding are not just that I happen to be interested in the book (I'm interested in lots of books, and I don't plan on responding to them all) or that I'm concerned about its religious impact on the beliefs of others. My concern is really a bit more prosaic. I know that a lot of people learn about the past from works of fiction or from film. Just as *The Da Vinci Code* was hitting its stride, for example, Mel Gibson's movie *The Passion of the Christ* made its own debut. It was a smash hit, principally among people who were both interested in the story of Jesus and uninformed of what the Gospels themselves have to say about it. How will such people, probably for the rest of their lives, think about Jesus' last hours? They'll think about them in light of what they saw portrayed on the big screen. Mel Gibson, much more than Matthew, Mark, Luke, or John, will affect how people understand Jesus' death, for at least the coming generation.

The ability of film directors and book authors to affect public sentiment and to shift public thinking is neither a good thing nor a bad one; it is simply a reality of the times. But when the images they create for their viewers or readers are *erroneous*—well, it means people misunderstand history as it really was and substitute fiction for facts. Maybe there's no real harm in that. But for those of us who spend our lives studying the history, it can grate a bit on the nerves.

And so I've decided to write up a response to Dan Brown's book, to deal not with the nature of the story (I loved it as a murder mystery) but with the nature of its historical claims about Jesus, Mary Magdalene, Constantine the Great, and the formation of the canon of scripture—all of them foundational issues for the story that Brown has created for us.

The way to begin is by giving a brief synopsis of the story as a refresher for those who have already read it (I'm assuming that anyone who might want to read this book will have already read Dan Brown's).

The Da Vinci Code: A Brief Synopsis

The Da Vinci Code has a complex and intricately woven plot, which I will give here in only brief form. There has been a mysterious murder, in Paris, of the renowned curator of the Louvre, Jacques Saunière. Because of bizarre religious symbols left at the scene of the crime, drawn by Saunière himself just before his death, a master of religious symbology, Robert Langdon, a professor at Harvard who is in Paris to deliver a lecture, is called in to investigate. He is joined by a police cryptographer, Sophie Neveu, who happens to be Saunière's granddaughter; she and her grandfather have been estranged for ten years. What Langdon and Neveu do not realize at first, but eventually come to learn, is that Saunière was the head of a secret religious group known throughout history as the Priory of Sion, which has always guarded the secret to the true nature and whereabouts of the Holy Grail.

A bizarre set of circumstances sets Langdon and Neveu on a search, following clues that Saunière has left behind, with the ultimate goal of finding the mysterious and long-sought Grail. Also in the pursuit, however, are those responsible for Saunière's death, who evidently have killed him while attempting to learn the whereabouts of the Grail. These mysterious others have used members of the fanatical Catholic order Opus Dei as pawns to lead them to the place of the Grail's hiding.

In the course of their adventures, Langdon and Neveu meet up with Sir Leigh Teabing, a wealthy aristocrat and expert on the Grail, who discusses the historical background to its mystery. The Grail is not the cup of Christ but the container that held his seed—it is in fact a person, Mary Magdalene, who was Jesus' wife and lover, who became pregnant by him and bore him a daughter. After his crucifixion, Mary and her child fled to France, and there the divine ancestral line of Christ was continued down through the ages.

There were secret documents kept about the existence of this bloodline of Christ. These documents celebrate the feminine principle in early Christianity and include a number of early Gospels that came to be suppressed by Christianity in the fourth century, specifically by the emperor Constantine. Constantine destroyed the eighty-some Gospels that were vying for a position in the New Testament, elevated Jesus from being a mere mortal to being the Son of God, and completely silenced the tradition about Mary and the divine feminine, demonizing the feminine in Christianity and destroying its true nature as a celebration of the feminine deity.

But the Priory of Sion has, for centuries, known the truth about Jesus and Mary and has long met in secret in order to celebrate their holy union and to worship the divine feminine. This secret society, of which Jacques Saunière was the most recent head, has kept the tomb of Mary Magdalene and the hundreds of documents that told the truth of the divine feminine.

Other famous people had headed the Priory of Sion and celebrated the truth of the marriage of Jesus and Mary—including notably Leonardo da Vinci, who painted Mary Magdalene in his famous fresco *The Last Supper* and gave hints of the truth of Jesus and Mary in many of his other works of art, there for those with the knowledge of the truth to see and revel in.

Langdon and Neveu, with the help of Sir Leigh Teabing, gradually unravel the mystery surrounding the Grail and the secret documents that reveal its true power as they follow an intricate maze of cryptograms that lead them from one place and puzzle to another—until they arrive at the truth of the Grail and the place of its final hiding.

The Historical Questions Raised

Even before I read *The Da Vinci Code* for myself, I had already been asked about it—in particular about its historical background. Is there any truth in what it says about Jesus and Mary Magdalene? Were there really secret Gospels that told the secret of their physical union? Were they really married? Did Mary really give birth to a child, whose holy lineage has been preserved down to today? Did the emperor Constantine suppress the other Gospels and create the Christian Bible? Did he eliminate the divine feminine from Christianity, promote the masculine Jesus to the realm of divinity, and so change the tenor of Christianity for all time?

These are the sorts of questions I will be addressing in the chapters that follow. I should be clear about what I will *not* be addressing. I will not be talking about the virtues of *The Da Vinci Code* as a piece of fiction—although I must say that I like it a lot and think, as I noted, that it's a terrific page-turner. I will not be talking about any of the modern claims it makes about Opus Dei, the Priory of Sion, or the role of the Vatican. Nor will I be considering the paintings and beliefs of Leonardo da Vinci.

My focus instead will be on the historical foundations of the book: the historical Jesus, the historical Mary, the development of the early Christian church, the writings of the early Christian Gospels, and the role played by Constantine in the formation of what has come down to us as the beliefs and scriptures of the Christian religion. How much of what is found in the historical background to this book is fact and how much fiction? How much truth is there in *The Da Vinci Code*?

In some ways the question is raised by *The Da Vinci Code* itself, as it begins (on p. 1, before the Prologue) with a list of items that it labels fact, including statements about the Priory of Sion, Opus Dei, and other items; here as well is included the claim "All descriptions of artwork, architecture, documents, and secret rituals in this novel are accurate."

But are they? I will not be dealing with art, architecture, or rituals. But I will be dealing with documents. And as we will see, even when Dan Brown strives to present facts (and indicates that he is providing them accurately), he has played with them—many of them are, in actuality, part of his fiction. It is the goal of my discussion to separate the fact from the fiction, the historical realities from the flights of fancy, for anyone interested in knowing about the historical beginnings of Christianity, especially in the life of Jesus and the writings that make up the New Testament.

How Critical History Gets Done

Before getting into this discussion I should say a brief word about how I plan to proceed. There are a variety of ways that one can approach the past, including the ancient past as it is recounted in a work of fiction such as *The Da Vinci Code*. Some people try creatively to imagine what the past was like, without basing their views on any actual (or very few) sources of information. Others take at face value whatever sources happen to survive, and try to meld them into some kind of synthesis. Both of these approaches are uncritical, in that they do not weigh and evaluate the surviving evidence. Our only access to the past is through sources that can tell us about it, yet our sources cannot simply be taken at face value because they often contradict one another and always represent their authors' perspectives, biases, and worldviews. And so the best way to try to reconstruct the past is by using our sources critically—that is, by doing critical history.

It is difficult for critical historians (or anyone) to reconstruct what actually happened in the past for the simple reason that the events of history can never be *proven*. That's because once something happens, it is over and done with, and it can't be summoned up to happen again. With my students I sometimes contrast the way critical historians work with the way empirical scientists do. Empirical sciences use repeated experimentation in order to establish proof. On an elementary level, if I want to *prove* that bars of iron sink in lukewarm water but bars of Ivory soap float, all I need to do is get a hundred tubs of lukewarm water and start tossing in the bars of iron and the bars of soap. Every time the iron will sink and the Ivory soap will float. This sets up a kind of predictive probability that we consider proof— namely, that if we do the same thing another time, the same result will occur.

History is not like that because the events of the past can never be repeated. And so other kinds of "proof"—other than controlled and repeated experiments—need to be used to establish levels of probability. And as with science, all history is a matter of probabilities. Some things are virtually certain (the Allies really did win World War II). Other things are highly probable but not as certain (George Washington did have false teeth). Other things are even less certain but still probable (Caesar did cross the Rubicon). Yet others are genuine question marks (was Mary Magdalene an intimate companion of Jesus?).

What makes some things more certain, or at least more probable, than others? In every case, it is the nature of the evidence. We have millions of eyewitnesses who can testify to the victory of the Allies in World War II. How many eyewitness reports do we have for Washington's dental health or Caesar's military activities? Very few indeed. What about Mary Magdalene and Jesus?

As it turns out, with respect to Mary Magdalene, a number of our sources come from the Bible. This raises another issue, one that will become important as we deal with the historical claims of *The Da Vinci Code*: how does the fact that an ancient source (for example, the Gospel of Mark) appears in the Bible affect its historical reliability? For critical historians, the sources in the Bible have to be treated like every other source from the past—they need to be examined critically to see if they are reliable or not. Among other things, this involves seeing how they stack up against other sources from the time—to see, for example, if they are contradicted by these other sources. If there are contradictions between sources, then the historian has to decide which ones to believe. And to make this decision the historian needs to have *reasons*. It isn't good enough to say that if something is stated in the Bible it is necessarily accurate. What if in the retelling of the story the biblical writer changed a historical event for reasons of his own? But on the other hand—and this is a point I need to stress—if there is a source that is outside the Bible that tells a different story (for example, the Gospel of Mary), *that* source is not necessarily right either. All sources need to be evaluated to see which ones are more reliable and which ones less so.

I am emphasizing this point because some people are inclined simply to believe anything found in a canonical source (whether it is the writings of Julius Caesar, George Washington, or the Bible), whereas others are inclined to believe anything that *contradicts* a canonical source. This latter approach is especially favored by people who are attracted to conspiracy theories—but also by intellectually curious people who believe the maxim that "the winners write the history" and are therefore intrigued by the possibility of recovering the "other side" of the story. Critical historians can't approach sources in that way, automatically favoring one side against the other. Instead, every source has to be carefully weighed and evaluated. And as we will see in a later chapter, this is true even for sources dealing with such an important figure as Jesus—whose story is told in books that made it into the New Testament as well as in books that did not (including some, such as the Gospel of Philip, that play an important role in *The Da Vinci Code*). The critical historian looks at *all* of these sources, comparing them carefully with one another, determining which ones can be trusted as reliable and which ones need to be taken with a pound of salt.

In this connection, I should point out that most of the records of the past—millions and millions of records, of every period of the past—no longer survive but remain lost to posterity. This includes the records of Jesus' life and the lives of his followers. We luckily have more sources available to us now for Jesus (and Mary Magdalene, for example) than scholars just a century ago probably even dreamed of. But still, we have a very small fraction of the sources that at one time or another must have existed. Some of the sources that did not survive were no doubt destroyed by

Christians who found their teachings to be offensive or wrong-headed. But most of them have not survived simply because at some point in the past, no one bothered to copy them any longer.

This final point is also worth stressing: the only written sources we have from the distant past come to us in handwritten copies (well before Gutenberg's invention of the printing press in the fifteenth century). It was not difficult to make a document disappear in antiquity; this could be accomplished simply by not having it copied. Contrary to the hints that one sees here or there among conspiracy literature about early Christianity—or even in historical fiction such as *The Da Vinci Code*—we have little evidence of mass burnings of "dangerous" books in antiquity. If a book was thought to be problematic, it simply wasn't reproduced. Luckily, some such "rare" books have turned up in modern times, thanks to discoveries made serendipitously and, on occasion, by trained archaeologists.

In the chapters that follow, as I assess the historical claims of *The Da Vinci Code*, I will take all our surviving sources into account, both canonical and noncanonical, orthodox and heretical, well known and virtually forgotten. It is only by considering such sources that we can come to a clear understanding about past figures that we are interested in knowing about, including three that figure so prominently for the plot of *The Da Vinci Code*: Jesus, Mary Magdalene, and the emperor Constantine.

Part One

The Emperor Constantine, the New Testament, and the Other Gospels

Chapter One

The Role of Constantine in Early Christianity

Despite the intricacies of its plots and subplots, *The Da Vinci Code* is essentially a story of right versus wrong, good versus evil. And so it is no surprise to find that characters can be lined up on these respective sides. Good characters include, of course, Robert Langdon and Sophie Neveu, who are pure in thought and intent only on discovering the truth. An ambiguously good character is the head of the French judicial police, Bezu Fache, a gruff figure whose actions often seem self-serving and arrogant but who in the end is seen to be on the side of the good. On the bad side we find, to our surprise, Leigh Teabing (the "Teacher"—before his self-disclosure Teabing appears to be on Langdon and Neveu's side of things); Rémy, Teabing's chauffeur and spy; and the albino monk Silas, who kills on demand in order to achieve what seems to him to be a greater good.

Not only characters in the narrative, however, but also the historical figures on which the story is based can be aligned with good and evil. Jesus and Mary Magdalene, of course, are good figures from the past. The archetypical bad guy, on the other hand, is the fourth-century Roman emperor Constantine. Constantine, in fact, is said to be at fault for many of the ills that came to plague the Christian religion from his day onward. According to Leigh Teabing (and to some extent Langdon), Constantine was the one who altered the form of Christianity for all time, emphasizing the masculine, demonizing the feminine, falsely attributing deity to the mortal prophet Jesus, and suppressing earlier Gospels that celebrated Jesus' humanity while canonizing texts that perceived him as divine. Is this portrayal true?

The Christianity of Constantine

More specifically, we learn from Teabing that Constantine never actually became a Christian but remained a pagan his entire life; Constantine simply used Christianity for his own political ends. He allegedly called the Council of Nicea in the year 325 in an attempt to unify Christianity by compelling it to acknowledge Jesus as a divine being rather than a human (prior to this time, Christians saw Jesus as human). And then Constantine created the Bible that we have today, a Bible in which the feminine is excluded and the masculine celebrated, in which the man Jesus is proclaimed divine.

How much historical reality is there to these claims about Constantine, and how much are they flights of fancy, fictions that support the narrative but are not grounded in history? We can start with the question of Constantine's own commitment to Christianity. Is it true that he remained a pagan for his entire life and never actually converted to Christianity?

Consider the key conversation between Sophie and Leigh Teabing on this point:

"I thought Constantine was a Christian," Sophie said.

"Hardly," Teabing scoffed. "He was a lifelong pagan who was baptized on his deathbed, too weak to protest. . . . Three centuries after the crucifixion of Jesus Christ, Christ's followers had multiplied exponentially. Christians and pagans began warring, and the conflict grew to such proportions that it threatened to rend Rome in two. Constantine decided something had to be done. In 325 A.D., he decided to unify Rome under a single religion, Christianity."

Sophie was surprised. "Why would a pagan emperor choose *Christianity* as the official religion?"

Teabing chuckled. "Constantine was a very good businessman. He could see that Christianity was on the rise, and he simply backed the winning horse." (p. 232)

Historians would recognize some truth in these claims, but on the whole, they are more fiction than fact. The first thing to consider is the course of Christianity leading up to the famous conversion of Constantine to the faith.

The Struggles Between Christians and Pagans

It is not true to say, as Teabing does, that "Christians and pagans began warring, and the conflict grew to such proportions that it threatened to rend Rome in two." This gives far too much credit to the strength of Christianity prior to Constantine's conversion, making it seem as though Christians were nearly as numerous as pagans and were constantly on the attack and counterattack. The reality is quite different. Christians prior to Constantine in the early fourth century were a small minority within the empire and were subject to persecution by the overwhelming majority groups—the pagans and their governmental authorities.

First I should probably say something about definitions. *Pagan*, when used in this context, is not a negative term. It simply refers to any of the adherents of the empire's polytheistic religions—that is, religions that worshiped many gods. And since everyone in the empire, with the exception of Jews and Christians, worshiped many gods, this included the vast bulk of the population.

The gods who were worshiped were of all kinds. There were the "great gods" that we know of from Greek and Roman mythology—for example, the Greek Zeus, Ares, and Athena, or their Roman counterparts Jupiter, Mars, and Minerva. But more than that there were gods of every locality and every function: gods who specially dwelt in and protected cities and towns throughout the empire (different gods for different places), gods of the family and household, gods of forests, streams, and fields, gods of various functions—those who made the crops grow, who kept the livestock fertile, who protected women in childbirth, who provided health and wealth and peace, who could do small favors for an individual when asked.

During this period of the Roman Empire there *was* a movement toward seeing one god as superior to others, as the God over all. Constantine himself was known to worship the "invincible sun god" (in Latin: Sol Invictus) before, and even after, becoming Christian. Sometimes Constantine, and others, appear to have identified this deity with the god Apollo, also associated with the sun. But once Constantine converted to Christianity, he appears to have thought that this god was really the Christian God.

In any event, the pagan religions of the empire worshiped many gods in ways that seemed appropriate to them. It is important to realize this to make sense of the interactions between Christians and pagans that Leigh Teabing makes reference to when he indicates that pagans and Christians were "warring" against one another. In fact, that's not exactly the case. There *were* violent struggles, but historically they were almost entirely one-sided. It was the pagan majority that was warring against the Christian minority, trying to wipe it out.

Christianity had been a persecuted religion from virtually the beginning.[1] The religion started, in fact, with the torture and execution of its founder, Jesus. And after his death a number of his followers met the same fate. Sometimes it was Jews who persecuted the early Christians, because in many Jews' view the Christians were committing blasphemy against God by calling Jesus the messiah. But as time went on, persecutions were increasingly undertaken by the Roman pagans and their administrative officials.

The reasons pagans hated Christians had to do with the pagan understanding of the gods. The gods provided the good things in life: health, prosperity, love, peace, fertility, and so on. They did this in simple exchange for worship—the sacrifice of an animal or other foodstuffs on occasion, and prayers said in their honor. These gods were not jealous of one another, insisting that worshipers adhere to the religious rites pertaining only to one or the other of them. All of them were gods, and all of them deserved to be worshiped. What happened, though, when they were not properly acknowledged? They could get angry, and when that happened, look out! The gods might retaliate with any manner of "natural" disasters: plague, famine, drought, earthquake. When these things occurred, the simplest explanation was that it was the gods who had brought them. And the reason was that they had not been paid proper attention. But who was it who refused to worship the gods in the ways they required? It was the Christians, who insisted that there was only one God, the God of Jesus, and that he alone was to be worshiped.[2]

When disasters struck towns, cities, or regions in the second and third Christian centuries, it could easily be believed that it was the Christians who were at fault. This sometimes led to mob violence against the Christians. And when that got out of hand, sometimes the Roman administrators had to intervene and apply official pressure to Christians to get them to recant their belief in the Christian God and to worship the pagan gods in the ways appropriate to them. When Christians refused, they were punished, sometimes with torture and death.

This is the actual situation of Christians and pagans in the empire. It was not, as Teabing asserts, a case of two warring factions. It was a case of a pagan majority persecuting a Christian minority. The persecutions against Christians, as it turns out, came to a head right before Constantine appeared on the scene. His predecessor as emperor was a man named Diocletian, who had control of the eastern part of the empire, while the west was controlled by a colleague named Maximian. Diocletian decided that the Christians (who probably made up something like 5–8 percent of the empire at the time) had to be dealt with once and for all. And so in 303 CE (CE stands for "Common Era," which scholars now use in place of AD) he, with Maximian cooperating, inaugurated an empire-wide persecution (most of the earlier persecutions, going back to the first century, were entirely local affairs, not empire-wide). Several imperial edicts were issued that called for the burning of Christian books, the demolition of Christian churches, the removal of class privileges for Christians, and eventually the imprisonment of high-ranking Christian clergy. In 304, a further edict required all Roman subjects to perform sacrifices to the gods; noncompliance meant death or forced labor. Christians, of course, could not comply without compromising their faith. This "Great Persecution," as it is called, lasted on and off for nearly a decade.

In Leigh Teabing's summary, Constantine was the one who brought the conflicts between pagans and Christians to an end in the year 325. This too is not correct. Constantine established peace from the Christian persecutions in 313 CE, the year after he converted. To make sense of how it all happened, we need to consider his conversion itself, which was a rather complicated affair. What is clear, however, is that, contrary to Teabing's assertion, Constantine did not remain a committed pagan his entire life. He himself marked his conversion with a decisive moment that occurred, as it turns out, on the battlefield.

The Conversion of Constantine

We unfortunately do not have reliable accounts of what *actually* happened when Constantine converted, only reports such as the one recorded by Constantine's religious biographer, Eusebius, a fourth-century Christian author who is sometimes known as the "father of church history," as he is the first Christian to write a comprehensive account of the church's history from the days of Jesus up to his own time, the time of Constantine. In addition to his ten-volume *History of the Church*, Eusebius wrote a biography of Constantine. As one might imagine, the biography is slanted toward Eusebius's own Christian perspective. But even so, he claims that he heard about Constantine's famous conversion from Constantine himself, some years later.[3]

The historical setting for the conversion, at any rate, is plain. After Diocletian voluntarily abdicated in 305 CE, Constantine became the emperor in his place; in Rome itself, however, Maximian laid claim to the imperial throne, until Constantine defeated him in battle. But then Maximian's son Maxentius took control in the city. Constantine was intent on being the sole ruler of the empire, and that meant disposing of Maxentius and his armies. Constantine marched on Rome, and there was a major battle at the Milvian Bridge over the Tiber River. Constantine later related a supernatural sign that occurred to him before the battle, a sign that eventually led him to embrace Christianity as the one true religion. According to his account, he knew that he would be victorious in the upcoming battle only if supported by divine power, but he was at a loss concerning which god to petition for aid in his struggle. But then he had a vision, in broad daylight. In the sky he saw a standard that was in the shape of a cross; above it were the words "By this sign, conquer."

Confused by what this could be mean, that night he dreamed that Christ came to him with the same sign and told him to use it as protection against his enemies. The next day Constantine described the sign to artisans he had summoned, and they constructed a lavish version of it from gold and precious stones. It was in the shape of the cross, with two Greek letters at the top, a chi and a rho—the first two letters of Christ's name. According to Eusebius, Constantine called in religious advisors who could explain what it all meant, and they told him that if he would commit himself to the worship of the Christian God, he would be protected in all things.

Under this sign, then, he engaged in battle at the Milvian Bridge with Maxentius and won a resounding victory, establishing himself as senior emperor of the west (another general, Licinius, was the emperor in the eastern part of the empire).

Leigh Teabing is right to intimate that from that moment on Constantine was not a tried-and-true Christian with nothing pagan left about him. For one thing, scholars have noted that he appears to have continued to worship the sun god even after his "conversion": coins minted in his reign, for example, continued to portray Sol Invictus for another nine years. It may be that Constantine conflated his older religion with his newfound faith in the Christian God. It is probably no accident that he determined that the Christian God was to be worshiped on the day of the sun (Sunday) and that the birth of Christ came to be celebrated at the time of the winter solstice. But in any event, contrary to Teabing's assertion, Constantine certainly began to see himself as a Christian in some sense, starting with this climactic moment in 312.

The next year, Constantine arranged with Licinius, his colleague who had control of the empire in the east, to proclaim an empire-wide cessation of hostilities against the Christians. This involved issuing an edict, known to history as the Edict of Milan, that provided for freedom of religion for all people in the empire, Christian, pagan, and Jew, to worship whichever god(s) they chose in ways appropriate to them. It was this—not a council called twelve years later in Nicea—that brought an end to the pagan-Christian conflicts.

Constantine identified himself, and others identified him, as a Christian from this point on, although, as I indicated, there did appear to remain vestiges of his former commitment to pagan deities for another decade or so. But by the early 320s Constantine was firmly committed to the Christian faith. Leigh Teabing is right to say that he was not actually baptized until he was on his deathbed (in 337 CE), but this was not an act conducted against his will, as Teabing implies. It was, in fact, not at all uncommon for Christians to wait to receive baptism until the very end. Long before this, however, Constantine had made his Christian commitments widely known, among other things by the benefactions that he poured out upon the Christian church and its clergy for well over twenty years.

The question remains of why Constantine converted to the Christian faith. Here it is hard to know if Teabing is right or

These pieces of marble are the remains of a monumental statue of the emperor Constantine dating from after 315 CE. The statue, which stood 9 meters high (the head pictured here is 2.6 meters), loomed in a massive new public structure in the city of Rome, the Basilica Nova. Construction of the basilica was begun under Maxentius, the rival emperor defeated by Constantine in 312. The installation of this monumental statue marked the triumphant presence of the new emperor in the ancient capital of the empire.

not, that Constantine decided simply to "back the winning horse." It is clear that Constantine was intent on unifying the empire that had been fractured for so long (during the fifty years before the accession of Diocletian, the empire had seen twenty different emperors). He took a series of financial and political steps to that end. And possibly by aligning himself with the Christian God he saw a way of bringing cultural unity to the empire: this could be one empire that worshiped the one God (the Christian

God, rather than the multifarious gods otherwise worshiped throughout the empire), with one emperor at its helm. One God, one faith, one emperor, one empire.

What is beyond dispute is that Constantine's conversion was one of the most significant events in the history of Western civilization. Christianity went from being a persecuted and much hated minority religion within the empire to being the religious preference of the emperor himself. Favors were showered on the church; it became exceedingly popular to become a Christian and thereby to renounce the pagan gods. Conversions happened in droves. By the end of the fourth century, Christians were the majority of the empire's population. All emperors after Constantine, with one brief exception, were Christian. Within fifty years of his death, Christianity was the official religion of the empire. As one writer has put it, Constantine's conversion was "the second greatest story ever told."[4]

But his conversion in 312 and his edict of toleration in 313 were not the end of the story. For, as Teabing himself indicates, something significant happened in the year 325. Teabing is mistaken to say that it was then that Constantine sought to unify his empire behind Christianity. That had already been in the process of happening. But there was a problem with using Christianity as a means of unification: the Christian church itself was *disunified* over several fundamental issues, none more important than its theological views. In order for Christianity to unify the empire, it had to unify itself. And that's the real reason Constantine called a council of Christian bishops (some 200–250 of them) to resolve problems that had been causing internal squabbles among the Christians; it met in the city of Nicea and is therefore called the Council of Nicea.

The Council of Nicea

Teabing mentions this council when speaking to Sophie Neveu
in his drawing room. He explains to her that Constantine's Council of Nicea was convened in order to vote on the divinity of
Jesus, as a way to consolidate the emperor's own power base.

> "During this fusion of religions, Constantine needed to strengthen
> the new Christian tradition, and held a famous ecumenical gath-
> ering known as the Council of Nicaea. . . . At this gathering,"
> Teabing said, "many aspects of Christianity were debated and
> voted upon—the date of Easter, the role of the bishops, the ad-
> ministration of sacraments, and, of course, the *divinity* of Jesus."
> "I don't follow. His divinity?"
> "My dear," Teabing declared, "until *that* moment in history,
> Jesus was viewed by His followers as a mortal prophet . . . a great
> and powerful man, but a *man* nonetheless. A mortal."
> "Not the Son of God?"
> "Right," Teabing said. "Jesus' establishment as 'the Son of God'
> was officially proposed and voted on by the Council of Nicaea."
> "Hold on. You're saying Jesus' divinity was the result of a *vote*?"
> "A relatively close vote at that," Teabing added. . . . "By offi-
> cially endorsing Jesus as the Son of God, Constantine turned
> Jesus into a deity who existed beyond the scope of the human
> world, an entity whose power was unchallengeable." (p. 233)

Once again, there are elements of both fact and fiction in
Teabing's view. Constantine did call the Council of Nicea, and
one of the issues involved Jesus' divinity. But this was not a council
that met to decide whether or not Jesus was divine, as Teabing
indicates. Quite the contrary: everyone at the Council—and in
fact, just about every Christian everywhere—already agreed that
Jesus was divine, the Son of God. The question being debated
was how to *understand* Jesus' divinity in light of the circumstance
that he was also human. Moreover, how could both Jesus and

God be God if there is only one God? *Those* were the issues that were addressed at Nicea, not whether or not Jesus was divine. And there certainly was no vote to determine Jesus' divinity: this was already a matter of common knowledge among Christians, and had been from the early years of the religion.

The Divinity and Humanity of Jesus

Teabing in fact presents a rather confused picture to Sophie in his discussion of Jesus' identity as divine. On one hand, he indicates that Jesus' divinity was not accepted until Nicea in the year 325; on the other hand, he indicates that Constantine accepted into his canon of scripture only those Gospels that portrayed Jesus as divine, eliminating all the other Gospels that portrayed Jesus as human. But if Jesus' divinity was not acknowledged by Christians until the council of Nicea (Teabing's view), how could the Gospels of Matthew, Mark, Luke, and John portray him as divine already in the first century (which is also his view)?

Even beyond this inconsistency, the view that Teabing lays out is wrong on all key points: Christians before Nicea already did accept Jesus as divine; the Gospels of the New Testament portray him as human as much as they portray him as divine; the Gospels that did *not* get included in the New Testament portray him as divine as much, or more so, than they portray him as human. I will deal with the first two points in this chapter, and the third in chapters to come.

Scholars who study the history of Christian theology will find it bizarre, at best, to hear Teabing claim that Christians before the Council of Nicea did not consider Jesus to be divine. Our earliest surviving Christian author is the apostle Paul, several of whose writings can be found in the New Testament. Paul was producing his letters about twenty or thirty years after Jesus' death (250 years *before* the Council of Nicea), and in them it becomes abundantly clear that Paul understands that Jesus Christ was in some sense divine. As he says in one of his earlier letters, the epistle to the Philippians:

> Have this same mind in yourselves which was in Christ Jesus, who although he was in the form of God, did not regard equality with God something to be grasped, but he emptied himself and took on the form of a slave, having come in the likeness of a human. (Phil. 2:5–7)

For Paul—and presumably for the Philippians to whom he wrote—Christ was "in the form" of God and was, in some sense, equal with God, even though he became human.

Similar teachings can be found in other writings of the New Testament. One of Jesus' common designations throughout these writings is "Son of God." This is scarcely an epithet that came to be applied to Jesus on the basis of a close vote at the Council of Nicea hundreds of years later! Our earliest Gospel, that of Mark, begins by announcing its subject matter: "The beginning of the Gospel of Jesus Christ, the son of God" (Mark 1:1).[5] The latest of our canonical Gospels, the Gospel of John, is even more explicit. Here Jesus is not merely the Son of God—although he is that as well (see e.g., John 1:18; 3:16, 18)—but in some sense is actually God himself.

So states the poem that begins this Gospel:

> In the beginning was the Word, and the Word was with God, and the *Word was God*. He was in the beginning with God. All things came into being because of him, and apart from him nothing came into being that came into being. (John 1:1–3)

And who, for John, is this "Word" that was in the beginning with God and in fact was himself God? There can be little question about who it is, for as he says at the end of this poem:

> And the Word became flesh and dwelt among us, and we have
> beheld his glory, glory as of the unique one before the Father,
> full of grace and truth. . . . For grace and truth have come to us
> through Jesus Christ. (1:14, 17)

For this author, already in the first century, Jesus Christ is identified as a divine being (the "Word") through whom God created the world, one who has completely revealed God to his people, since he himself was a divine being come down from heaven and made flesh.

That is why Jesus can claim equality with God in this Gospel. As he puts it in one place: "I and the Father are one" (10:30). And that is why his followers in this Gospel recognize his divine identity, including doubting Thomas at the end of the story, who sees Jesus raised from the dead and proclaims, "My Lord and my God!" (20:28).

This view of Jesus as divine is not restricted to Paul and the Gospels, however. It is the common view held among Christian writers of the early centuries. As one of our earliest writers outside of the New Testament, the Christian martyr Ignatius of Antioch (d. 110 CE), put it in his own poetic way:

> There is one physician, both fleshly and spiritual, born and
> unborn, God come in the flesh, true life in death, from both
> Mary and God, first subject to suffering and then beyond suffer-
> ing, Jesus Christ our Lord. (Ignatius, *To the Ephesians*, 7.2)

From the very beginning—as far back as we have Christian writings (long before Constantine)—it became commonplace to understand that Jesus was in some sense divine. But there was always a stumbling block, because most Christians understood as well that Jesus was also human. How could he be human if he was divine? That is a question that Christians struggled with for centuries, and in a sense it was the question that the Council of Nicea was called to resolve.

Before discussing the immediate problem that led to the calling of the council, however, I should stress the fact that most early Christians understood Jesus in both ways, as human and divine. I need to emphasize the point because in *The Da Vinci Code*, Teabing indicates that all Christians before Nicea understood Jesus as human and not divine—with the exception, evidently, of the authors of the four Gospels that made it into the New Testament, who portray him, according to Teabing, as only divine. As already indicated, this is wrong on all points. But it is especially wrong in thinking that the New Testament Gospels do not think of Jesus as human. Quite the contrary: Jesus is very much human in these books, as even a straightforward reading of the Gospels will make clear.

In our earliest Gospel, that of Mark, Jesus is, to be sure, called the Son of God. But he is principally portrayed as a Jewish prophet like other Jewish prophets. He has a fully human life (there is no word of a miraculous birth in this particular Gospel), he eats, he drinks, he gets angry, he experiences agony, he suffers, he bleeds, and he dies. He is nothing if not human here. The same can be said of all our Gospels, even the Gospel of John, which goes further than the others in portraying Jesus as divine. Even here Jesus is fully human, getting tired, hungry, sad, and so on.

Resolving the Tension of Jesus' Humanity and Divinity

Given the fact that our earliest sources portray Jesus as both divine and human, how do they resolve the difficulty? How, that is, can Jesus be God if he is also a man? This is a problem that Christians struggled with, for they recognized that humanity and divinity are two different things: God can't be a man any more than a man can be a rock.

Different early Christians had different ways of resolving this problem. Some, to be sure, argued that Jesus was so much human that he wasn't actually divine, and others argued that he was so much divine that he wasn't actually human. Both of these views, however, came to be seen in the second century as heresies (i.e., false teachings). An example of the first option can be seen among a second-century group of Christians known to scholars as the "adoptionists." These people maintained that Jesus was human in every way—he was born of the sexual union of Joseph and Mary, born the way everyone else is born. The one thing that made Jesus different from others, according to these adoptionists, was that he was more righteous than all others. As a result of his superior righteousness, God appointed him to be his "Son"—adopted him, in fact, at his baptism, where a voice came from heaven declaring, "You are my Son, today I have begotten you" (see Ps. 2:7). As a human adopted to be God's son, according to these adoptionist Christians, Jesus was given the divine mission to die as a sacrifice for the sins of others. This he did, in faithful fulfillment of God's command. As a reward for Jesus' faithfulness, God raised him from the dead and exalted him to his right hand, where he now lives in power, waiting for his return in judgment on the earth.

Christians today might be puzzled by this view and wonder why these adoptionist Christians didn't simply read their New Testaments to see that their views were wrong (since Jesus was born of a virgin and was himself actually the son of God). The reason they didn't read their New Testaments, though, is clear. There *was* no New Testament yet. To be sure, all the books of the New Testament (the writings of Paul and the Gospels, for example), had been written. But they weren't yet collected into a canon of scripture and called the New Testament. The formation of the canon came as a *result* of the controversies, including the controversies over Jesus' identity in the early centuries.

There were other Christians of the second and third centuries who took the opposite line, who insisted that Jesus was so fully divine that he could not actually be human. Sometimes these believers are called "docetists" (from the Greek word *dokeo*, which means "to seem" or "to appear"), because they maintained that Jesus wasn't human but only seemed to be. He was fully God. Jesus, then, only seemed to have human flesh and blood, human emotions, human frailties, and the human ability to suffer and die. In fact it was all an appearance.

Most Christians rejected the views of both the adoptionists and the docetists and insisted that in some sense Jesus was both human (as the adoptionists maintained) and divine (as the docetists claimed). But how could he be both things at once? Here is where different early Christians had some of their most interesting disagreements among themselves, and it was these disagreements that eventually led to the Council of Nicea.

Before that time there were some intriguing solutions to the problem of how Jesus could be both things at once, and to the related problem of how he could be God while God the Father is God, and yet there are not two Gods but only one. How could that be? One early solution was to say that Jesus was actually God the Father himself, who became a human. That way Jesus was both God and man (because he really did become a human), and there was still only one God even though Jesus was God and God was God, for they are one and the same.

This view eventually came to be labeled a heresy, however (as did the views of the adoptionists and docetists), for several reasons. Its opponents pointed out that God the Father was superior to all things and above such limitations as mortality, suffering, and death. To say that Jesus is God the Father, though, would be to say that God the Father *suffered*. The opponents of this view called it Patripassianism ("the Father suffers") and ridiculed it out of court. They pointed out, for example, that when Jesus prayed (see John 17), he obviously wasn't talking to himself.

But how, then, could he be God and human at the same time? And how could he and God (and the Spirit) be God if there was only one God? Very few Christians were willing to say there was more than one God—that was a pagan view. So how could they remain monotheists while acknowledging the deity of Christ?

Arius and the Council of Nicea

One solution to this problem eventually led to the Council of Nicea. In the early fourth century, at about the time of Constantine's conversion, there was a popular teacher named Arius in Alexandria, Egypt, an important center of Christendom.[6] Arius tried to resolve the problem of the identity of Christ by maintaining that in the beginning there was only God the Father. But at some point in eternity past, God brought his Son into existence, and it was through this Son of God, Christ, that he created all things. Christ, then, was a divine being—but he was subordinate to God the Father as his first creation. And Christ was the one who brought into existence all else. He then became a human by being born of the Virgin; he died for sins, was raised from the dead, and continues to dwell with God, as God's own Son, in heaven.

This solution to the problem of Christ's identity was extremely popular, in part because it preserved so well all the affirmations that Christians wanted to make about God (there is only one God; he is manifest to us in Christ) and about Christ (he is divine; he became human). But there were other Christians who took serious issue with it, because in their view this made Christ subservient to God the Father and not fully God himself. One of the opponents of Arius was a young deacon in the Alexandrian church who was to become one of the most important figures in the history of fourth-century Christianity, a man named Athanasius. Athanasius and his co-religionists insisted on a paradoxical understanding of Christ as divine yet human. Christ had always existed—he did not come into being at a point in time—and he was himself fully (not derivatively) divine. He was, in fact, of the same essence as God the Father himself. This is the view that ultimately led to the orthodox doctrine of the Trinity, which maintains that there are in fact three persons who make up the one God. All three are equal in substance and are co-eternal, but the three do not make up three Gods: God is one, manifest in three persons.

This may seem to us today to be a rather arcane set of debates. But in Alexandria, and in other parts of the Christian world of the early fourth century, they were hotly contested. And the heat of the debates affected the unity of the church, as arguments, fights, and even acts of violence eventually broke out over the issue of whether Jesus was only "like" God, in that he was created as a secondary divinity, or was "of the same substance" as God, co-eternal with him. Later theologians, looking back, pointed out that the two positions that were being fought over amounted to no more than a difference over the letter *i*: one view said Jesus was like God (Greek *homoiousios*) and the other that he was of the same substance as God (Greek *homoousios*). But that *i* packed a real punch in its day.

What has all this to do with Constantine? As we have seen—and as Leigh Teabing himself indicates—Constantine wanted Christianity to help unify his empire. But how could Christianity bring unity when it was split against itself on what was considered at the time a fundamental theological issue (in some ways *the* theological issue): the nature of God himself? Constantine, wanting unity in the church because he wanted unity in his empire, called a council to decide the issue raised most poignantly by Arius, whether Christ was a divine creation of the Father or was himself co-eternal and equal with God.

The Council of Nicea met in 325 CE to decide the issue.[7] Contrary to what Leigh Teabing asserts, it was not a particularly close "vote." The vast majority of the 200 or 250 bishops present sided with the view of Athanasius against Arius, which was eventually to become the view of Christianity at large (although the debates continued for decades even after the council). And more important, contrary to Teabing, it was not a vote on Jesus' divinity. Christians for 250 years had agreed that Jesus was divine. The only question was *how* he was divine, and that was what the Council of Nicea was called to resolve.

Constantine According to Teabing

There are other comments that Teabing makes about the emperor Constantine that we will need to consider in later chapters. He argues, for example, that the Christian Bible as we have it—the twenty-seven books of the New Testament—were put together by Constantine himself in an effort to guarantee the unity of the church, which he sought as a unifying force in his empire. This claim, we will see, is completely wrong; the formation of the New Testament canon was a long, drawn-out process that began centuries before Constantine and was not completed until well after his death. He in fact had nothing to do with it. Among other things, the four Gospels we consider to be part of the New Testament were already firmly ensconced well before Constantine's conversion, and the "other" Gospels had already long been proscribed by Christian leaders as heretical productions—they weren't suppressed by Constantine.

Moreover, Teabing argues that Constantine shaped a masculinized form of the Christian religion, suppressing and even demonizing the feminine, so the true form of Christianity, which celebrated the divine feminine, came to be lost to posterity, except as it lived on in such marginalized secret societies as the Priory of Sion. As we will see, this too has no semblance of historical reality but instead marks another flight of fancy, useful for the fiction of *The Da Vinci Code* but bearing no relation to history as it actually happened.

Before getting to these issues, however, it will be important for us to consider the other documents from early Christianity that Teabing, and to a lesser degree Robert Langdon, refers to in *The Da Vinci Code*. These are documents now known through the recent discoveries of the Dead Sea Scrolls and the Nag Hammadi Library, which enlighten us concerning the true nature of Christianity. These will be the subject of the next chapter.

Chapter Two

The Discoveries of the Dead Sea Scrolls
and the Nag Hammadi Library

As Leigh Teabing explains the "real" nature of Christ to Sophie Neveu in his drawing room, he points out that even though the Gospels of the New Testament portray Jesus as divine and not human (a view that, as we have seen, is itself wrong), there were other Gospels from early Christianity that provide a more historically accurate portrayal, in which Jesus is seen as human. These Gospels, he tells her, have been discovered in relatively recent times, in the archaeological finds of the Dead Sea Scrolls and the documents unearthed near Nag Hammadi, Egypt. These, he indicates, are among the earliest surviving Gospel accounts of Jesus and can be used to correct the canonical view of him as divine.

Are these assertions about the Dead Sea Scrolls and the Nag Hammadi Library (as it is called) true? Or are they parts of the fiction of *The Da Vinci Code*?

Consider Teabing's words to Sophie:

> "Fortunately for historians," Teabing said, "some of the gospels that Constantine attempted to eradicate managed to survive. The Dead Sea Scrolls were found in the 1950s hidden in a cave near Qumran in the Judean desert. And, of course, the Coptic

Scrolls in 1945 at Nag Hammadi. In addition to telling the true Grail story, these documents speak of Christ's ministry in very human terms. Of course, the Vatican, in keeping with their tradition of misinformation, tried very hard to suppress the release of these scrolls." (p. 234)

Unfortunately, much of what Teabing says is historically inaccurate. (1) As we will later see, Constantine did not attempt to eradicate any of the earlier Gospels. (2) The Dead Sea Scrolls do not contain any Gospels, or in fact any documents that speak of Christ or Christianity at all; they are Jewish. (3) Their (initial) discovery was in 1947, not the 1950s. (4) The Coptic documents at Nag Hammadi were in book form, they were not scrolls (an important distinction for the history of early Christian books). (5) Neither these nor the Dead Sea Scrolls ever speak of the Grail story.[1] (6) Nor do they speak of Jesus' ministry "in very human terms"; if anything, Jesus is portrayed as more divine in the Nag Hammadi sources than he is in the Gospels of the New Testament. (7) The Vatican had nothing to do with covering up either of these discoveries.

That is not to say that the discoveries of the Dead Sea Scrolls and the Nag Hammadi Library are of no importance for the understanding of the historical Jesus and the stories told about him. Quite the contrary: both discoveries were immensely important, but not for the reasons that Teabing presents. To get a full appreciation of the importance of these findings, we need to consider them separately, starting with the more famous of the two, the Dead Sea Scrolls.

The Dead Sea Scrolls

The Discovery

There can be little doubt that the Dead Sea Scrolls were the most significant discovery of manuscripts in modern times.[2] The tale of their discovery is an interesting one, as it involved pure serendipity. In early 1947 a Bedouin shepherd boy named Muhammad edh-Dhib (which means "Muhammad the Wolf") was driving a flock of sheep and goats to a watering spring in the Judean desert, near the ancient ruins known as Qumran, by the northwest shore of the Dead Sea, about seven miles south of Jericho and twelve miles east of Jerusalem. One of his flock had strayed, and he went off in search of it. Spying a cave above him in the cliff face, he tossed a rock inside and heard it plunk against something. The next day he and a friend went back to investigate, and inside the cave they found large earthenware jars with intact scrolls inside, wrapped in linen.

When they informed their elders about the find, the earthenware jars and their contents were collected. These Bedouin realized that such things could be worth money, and they planned to sell them. The jars contained seven complete scrolls, and these were eventually sold in two lots, four of them to the Syrian Orthodox archbishop of Jerusalem and three to a scholar at Jerusalem's Hebrew University. Eventually the first lot of four was purchased by the young state of Israel (in 1955), leaving all of the original scrolls in the hands of Israeli authorities.

But the Bedouin realized that if this one cave yielded ancient treasures, other caves in the area might as well. There are, in fact, nearly three hundred caves and holes in the immediate vicinity. They were all searched, both by Bedouin and by trained archaeologists in the 1950s. Eleven of the caves, as it turns out, contained manuscript remains, most of them not intact, as the original seven had been, but in fragmentary form. One of the caves, called Cave 4 (since it was the fourth cave in which manuscripts were discovered), was chock full of scraps of manuscripts that had deteriorated over time—some fifteen thousand scraps from something like an original six hundred manuscripts. Piecing these together was quite a task, something like assembling six hundred jigsaw puzzles with most of their pieces missing and the surviving pieces being thrown haphazardly together.

But the task was well worth the effort. For these documents—both the original seven and the other manuscripts and manuscript fragments discovered in the other caves—were very ancient; many of them were otherwise unknown documents from ancient Judaism. The manuscripts, in fact, are some two thousand years old. They were created and used by a sect of Jews who were probably living at about the time of Jesus in a settlement at what is now the ruins called Qumran, near the caves.

This find is highly significant because it can provide us with crucial information about what was happening in Judaism in the centuries just before and after the beginning of the Christian era. And they are significant for understanding Christianity as well—not, as Teabing indicates, because they contain Gospels about Jesus, but because they can inform us about the Judaism of his day.

The Contents of the Scrolls

What kinds of books are represented among the manuscripts discovered in these eleven caves near the settlement of Qumran? The first thing to stress, again, is that there are no Christian documents of any kind here: these are all Jewish texts, made by Jews, copied by Jews, and used by Jews round about the time of Jesus (circa 150 BCE–70 CE).[3]

Among the most significant documents in the Dead Sea Scrolls are copies of the Hebrew Bible (the Christian Old Testament). Some of these copies are nearly complete—for example, one of the original seven from Cave 1 is a scroll of the prophet Isaiah.

Some of the caves (*above*), in the wilderness west of the Dead Sea near the Qumran community, in which the Dead Sea Scrolls (*two shown at left*) were found.

Every book of the Hebrew Bible is represented among the manuscripts discovered in the eleven caves, with the exception of the book of Esther. This discovery of biblical manuscripts is significant because prior to this, our oldest copy of the Hebrew Bible came from 1000 CE; these copies among the Dead Sea Scrolls were a millennium or more older than anything previously known to exist. And so we are able to tell how faithfully the texts of the Hebrew Bible were copied over the ages. As it turns out, some of the texts (for example, Isaiah) were copied with high accuracy, century after century; others (including the books of Samuel, for example), experienced significantly greater change with the passing of time.

Most of the other books discovered in the caves near Qumran were previously unknown to us—a veritable library of Jewish texts previously unavailable. They are mainly written in Hebrew (the language of the Jewish Scriptures), with some in Aramaic (the everyday spoken language of the time) and a very few in Greek (the language of international commerce and culture). They include commentaries written on the biblical texts, in which the authors interpret the text and explain its significance for the ongoing life of their own community. These commentaries are not particularly interested in showing what the biblical author may have wanted to communicate to his readers in his own day; they instead try to show how the biblical authors told prophecies that were being fulfilled many centuries later in the Qumran community itself.

There are other books among the Qumran documents that scholars have labeled "sectarian," meaning that they involve the life of the community itself—giving the rules of conduct, the entrance requirements, the penalties for violating the community's policies, and so on. Scholars are by and large convinced that this community was made up of a group of Jews known in other ancient sources as the Essenes. Reading these books, it becomes clear that this Essene community was filled with single, celibate men who had devoted their lives to purity in light of their belief that they were living at the end of time. Soon, they believed, God would intervene in history to overthrow the forces of evil and to reward his righteous ones.

Other books are filled with the community's prayers and psalms—books of poetry much like the Psalms of the Hebrew

Bible. Other books are concerned with strict interpretations of the laws of Moses, showing how these laws are to be understood and followed by members of the community. Yet other books are visionary in nature, indicating what will happen at the end of time when the forces of good (on the side of the members of the community) do battle with the forces of evil (the Devil and his earthly representatives—e.g., the Roman armies), overcoming them prior to the appearance of God's kingdom on earth.

All in all, these were highly significant discoveries for understanding Judaism in the days of Jesus—even if they never refer to Jesus himself or his followers, contrary to the claims of Leigh Teabing.

Arguably the most important feature of the Dead Sea Scrolls is that they highlight the centrality of Jewish apocalypticism for the milieu of Jesus. Because of the importance of apocalyptic thought for understanding Jesus (the subject of a later chapter in this book) and potentially for making sense of his relationship with women (a key feature of *The Da Vinci Code*), I should spend some time explaining what apocalypticism was, as we now know from the Dead Sea Scrolls and other Jewish documents from roughly the same time.

The Dead Sea Scrolls and Jewish Apocalypticism

Apocalypticism is a term modern scholars use for an ancient worldview. The term comes from the Greek word *apocalypsis*, which means "uncovering" or "unveiling." Those who subscribed to this worldview maintained that God had "unveiled" to them the heavenly secrets that could help them make sense of earthly realities; in particular, God had revealed to them what would happen in the near future when he intervened to destroy the evil in the world and establish his good kingdom.

There were Jewish apocalypticists in all walks of life around the time of Jesus. Some of them were members of sectarian communities such as the Essenes, others of them were Pharisees, some were prophetic figures (such as John the Baptist) and their followers, and yet others were Jews connected with no party but who simply shared this worldview (just as there are Christians today who don't belong to one denomination or another).

Whatever their party affiliation, apocalypticists, as seen from the Dead Sea Scrolls and other ancient Jewish documents, appear by and large to have subscribed to four major tenets:

1. *Dualism.* Jewish apocalypticists maintained that there were two fundamental components to reality: the forces of good and the forces of evil. On the side of good, of course, was God himself. But according to apocalypticists, God had a personal enemy, the Devil (prior to the advent of apocalypticism, there is no reference to the Devil in Jewish texts—for example, in most of the Hebrew Bible). God has his agents, the holy angels, and the Devil has his, the demons. On the side of God are superhuman powers such as righteousness and life; on the side of the Devil are the powers of sin and death. These are understood by apocalypticists to be actual powers in the world. Sin is not simply a bad thing that we sometimes do. For apocalypticists, sin is a cosmic force, aligned against God, that attempts to snare people and compel them to act in ways contrary to God. Why is it that some people "just can't stop themselves" from doing what they know is wrong? It is because sin has enslaved them. Death as well is not simply what happens when you stop breathing or your mind stops working; it is a cosmic force in the world that is trying to capture you, and when it succeeds, it annihilates you.

For Jewish apocalypticists, everything and everybody in the world sides with either the forces of good or the forces of evil.

There is no neutral ground, no gray territory, and so everyone has to choose.

Moreover, for apocalypticists this cosmic dualism gets worked out in a historical scenario, in that there is a radical disjunction between this age and the age to come. This age is controlled by the forces of evil. That is why there is so much pain and suffering in the world—famine, disease, war, and natural disasters, not to mention the more mundane experiences of hatred, loneliness, and death itself. But in the age to come all that is evil will be destroyed and only the good will be found; there will be no more hunger, heartache, suffering, pain, or death—only what God ordains, as he rules supreme here on earth.

2. *Pessimism*. Since apocalypticists maintained that the present age was evil, they had no hope that we can improve our lot in the here and now. Things are bad now, and they will only get worse, as the Devil and his minions acquire more and more power. We cannot make things better by improving our welfare system, putting more teachers in the classroom, or increasing the number of cops on the beat. The forces of evil are gaining in power and will continue to do so until the end of this age, when, literally, all hell will break out.

3. *Vindication*. But the end of this age is not the end of the story. For when things get just as bad as they can possibly get, God will then intervene on behalf of those who have sided with him. He will overthrow all the forces of evil in a cataclysmic act of judgment, destroying the Devil and all his powers and bringing his good kingdom here on earth.

Part of this vindication of God's holy ones will involve a resurrection of the dead. That is to say, God's judgment will come not only to those who happen to be alive at the time; it will affect all people, even those who have died, for the dead will be physically raised and forced to face judgment. And so people should not think that they can side with the forces of evil in this life to acquire prosperity and power, and then die and get away with it. They *can't* get away with it, because God will raise them from the dead and force them to face eternal punishment for the evils they've done, and there's not a sweet thing they can do to stop him.

On the other hand, those who have sided with God and suffered in this age as a result (and that *will* be the result of siding with the good, since it is the evil powers that are in control of this world) will be raised from the dead and given their eternal reward. And so people who are suffering now can look forward to being vindicated then, in the good kingdom that is coming. But when will this be?

4. *Imminence.* Jewish apocalypticists maintained that this final act of judgment was going to happen very soon. It was right around the corner. It was almost here. Apocalypticists believed that things were about as bad as they could possibly get, and God was soon to intervene and overthrow the forces of evil to bring in his kingdom. How soon would it be? "Truly I tell you, some of you standing here will not taste death before they see the Kingdom of God having come in power." These are the words of Jesus (Mark 9:1). Jesus himself, you see, was a Jewish apocalypticist, with views similar to those of the Essenes in the Dead Sea Scroll community, even though he was not a member of the community or, probably, ever had any contact with them. He says elsewhere, "Truly I tell you, this generation will not pass away before all these things take place" (Mark 13:30).

Jesus thus shared an apocalyptic view with the Essenes at Qumran. He differed from them in many ways as well—which is why scholars are virtually unanimous in thinking that he never belonged to their community. The Essenes at Qumran, for example, were intent on preserving their own purity by removing themselves from the polluting influences of the world around them; Jesus, on the other hand, was constantly surrounding himself with "tax collectors and sinners," concerned not for his personal purity nor for the rigorous adherence to the laws of Moses that the Essenes urged. Quite the contrary: he was frequently accused of having a rather lax attitude toward the law (for example, the law of Sabbath observance). But in a fundamental way he was like the members of the Dead Sea Scrolls community. He too was a dualist believing in the forces of good and evil (he is constantly shown combating demons, for example), in the imminent appearance of the kingdom of God (Mark 1:15; 9:1; 13:30), in the future resurrection of the dead, and so on.

To this extent Leigh Teabing is right: the Dead Sea Scrolls do help illuminate the true nature of Jesus. But it is not, as Teabing claims, because the scrolls contain anything explicitly Christian. They are thoroughly and completely Jewish. And it is not because they contain Gospels that are more accurate than those of the New Testament. There are in fact no Gospels among the hundreds of documents found at Qumran. And it is not because their accounts of Jesus portray him in a more human way than the Gospels of the New Testament. The scrolls say nothing about Jesus at all. They illuminate Jesus' character because they illuminate the Jewish milieu out of which Jesus and the earliest Christians emerged, a milieu filled with apocalyptic expectation that this evil age was drawing to a rapid close and that God was soon to intervene in judgment on this world before bringing in his good, eternal kingdom.

The Nag Hammadi Library

In *The Da Vinci Code*, when Leigh Teabing tries to convince Sophie Neveu that the earliest records of Christ portray him in human rather than divine terms, he shows her some of the actual proof. They are discussing the matter in his study, and he pulls from his shelf a book called *The Gnostic Gospels*, which is said to contain "photographs of what appeared to be magnified passages of ancient documents." He then informs Sophie, "These are photocopies of the Nag Hammadi and Dead Sea scrolls . . . the earliest Christian records" (p. 245).

We have already seen that the Dead Sea Scrolls are not in fact among the earliest Christian records. I should also point out that the book Teabing is referring to, *The Gnostic Gospels*, does not contain photographs of ancient documents at all, but is a study of the Nag Hammadi texts by the best-selling author Elaine Pagels (who is also quoted at length in the Dan Burstein book I referred to earlier, *Secrets of the Code*). All the same, Teabing makes an important point: the discovery of the Nag Hammadi Library did contain Gnostic writings, and some of these are significant for understanding how Jesus was portrayed in the early Church. As it turns out, however, this is not a portrayal of Jesus in human terms at all.

Once again we do well to start at the beginning by considering how the Nag Hammadi Library was discovered in the first place. Since this discovery is more central to the claims of *The Da Vinci Code* than the Dead Sea Scrolls, I will cover it in a bit more detail. This too was a completely serendipitous find, with similarities to the discovery of the Dead Sea Scrolls. But it took place a year and a half earlier and in a different part of the world—not in the wilderness of Judea near the Dead Sea but in the wilderness of Egypt near the Nile.

The Discovery

The find occurred in December 1945 when seven Bedouin field hands were digging for *sabakh*, a nitrate-rich fertilizer, near the cliff called Jabal al-Tarif along the Nile in Upper Egypt.[4] The fertilizer was used for the crops they grew near their small hamlet of al-Qasr, across the river from the largest village of the area, Nag Hammadi, some three hundred miles south of Cairo and forty miles north of Luxor and the Valley of the Kings. The leader of the group, the one responsible for the find once it was made and the one who later divulged the details of the discovery, was named, memorably enough, Mohammed Ali. It was Ali's younger brother, though, who actually made the find, accidentally striking something hard below the dirt with his mattock. It turns out to have been a human skeleton.[5] Digging around a bit, they uncovered next to the skeleton a large earthenware jar, about two feet high, with a bowl over the top, sealed with bitumen.

Mohammed Ali and his companions were reluctant to open the jar, for fear that it might contain an evil genie. On further reflection, they realized it might also contain gold, and so without further ado they smashed into it with their mattocks. No genie and no gold—just a bunch of old leather-bound books, of little use to a group of illiterate Bedouin.

Ali divided up the find, ripping the books apart so everyone would get a fair share. The others evidently wanted no part of them, though, and so he wrapped the lot in his turban, returned home, and deposited them in the outbuilding where they kept the animals. That night, his mother evidently used some of the brittle leaves to start the fire for the evening meal.

The story gets a bit complicated at this point, as real life intrudes, but in an almost unreal way. Mohammed Ali and his family had for a long time been involved in a blood feud with a tribe in a neighboring village. It had started some six months earlier, when Ali's father, while serving as a night watchman over some imported German irrigation machinery, had shot and killed an intruder. By the next day, Ali's father had himself been murdered by the intruder's family. Several weeks after they discovered the old books in the jar, Mohammed Ali and his brothers were told that their father's murderer was asleep by the side of the road, next to a pot of sugarcane molasses. They grabbed their mattocks, found the fellow still asleep, and hacked him to death. They then ripped open his chest, pulled out his still warm heart, and ate it—the ultimate act of blood vengeance.

The downside of the story—well, actually, there were a lot of downsides—was that the fellow they had murdered was the son of a local sheriff. By this time, Mohammed Ali had come to think that perhaps these old books they had found might be worth something, and he was afraid that as he and his brothers would be prime suspects in this cold-blooded murder, his house would be searched for clues. He gave one of the books to the local Coptic priest for safekeeping until the storm blew over.

As it turns out, this local priest had a brother-in-law who was an itinerant teacher of English and history, who stayed in his home once a week while making his rounds in the parochial schools in the area. The history teacher realized that in fact the book might be a significant find—significant enough to make some money—and went to Cairo to try to sell it. It was not an altogether successful attempt: the book was confiscated by the authorities. Eventually, though, he was allowed to sell it to the Coptic Museum.

The director of the museum had a good idea what the book was, and to make a long story short, in conjunction with a young visiting French scholar of antiquity, Jean Doresse, whom he had known in Paris—known fairly well, in fact, as he had proposed

THE DEAD SEA SCROLLS AND THE NAG HAMMADI LIBRARY   39

marriage to Mrs. Doresse before she became Mrs. Doresse—
the director managed to track down most of the remaining volumes and acquire them for the museum.

The Contents of the Collection

What was this ancient collection of books? The short answer is
that it is the most significant collection of lost Christian writings
to turn up in modern times, a total of forty-six different treatises,
most of them previously unknown.[6] It included several Gospels
about Jesus that had never before been seen by any Western
scholar, books known to have existed in antiquity but lost for nearly
fifteen hundred years, including Gospels about Jesus ostensibly
by such personages as his disciple Philip (which Leigh Teabing
quotes when discussing the importance of Mary Magdalene),
mystical speculations about the beginning of the divine realm and
the creation of the world, metaphysical reflections on the meaning of existence and the glories of salvation, expositions of important religious doctrines, and polemical attacks on other Christians
for their wrongheaded and heretical views.

The documents are written in Coptic, an ancient Egyptian language. But there are solid reasons for thinking that each was originally composed in Greek. The leather-bound books themselves
were manufactured in the second half of the fourth century. We
know this because the spines of the leather bindings were strength-
ened with scrap paper, and some of the scrap paper came from
receipts dated 341, 346, and 348 CE. The books thus must have
been manufactured sometime after 348 CE.

The date of the books, of course, is not the same as the date of
the documents found within the books—just as the Bible lying
on my desk was manufactured in 1998, but the documents it
contains were written some nineteen hundred years earlier. So

too with the Nag Hammadi texts: they were originally composed long before the end of the fourth century, when these particular books were made. Most of them appear to have been in existence by the second Christian century at the latest.

We don't know exactly who wrote these books or why they came to be hidden under the cliff of Jabal al-Tarif, just above the bend of the Nile, north of Luxor. It is significant that a Christian monastery, founded by the famous Christian monk Saint Pachomius in the fourth century, is located just three miles away. Scholars have been inclined to think that these books may have come from the library of the monastery, a view supported by the contents of the scrap paper in their bindings. But why would monks have disposed of the books?

As we will see more fully in a later chapter, a significant moment occurred in the history of the formation of the New Testament canon in the late fourth century. It was in 367 CE that the powerful bishop of Alexandria, Athanasius, whom we met in the previous chapter, wrote a letter to the churches throughout Egypt under his jurisdiction, in which he laid out in strict terms the contours of the canon of scripture.[7] This was the first time anyone of record had indicated that the twenty-seven books that we now have in our canon, and only those twenty-seven books, should be considered as scripture. Moreover, Athanasius insisted that other, "heretical" books not be read. Is it possible that monks of the Pachomian monastery near Nag Hammadi felt the heat from on high and cleaned out their library to conform with the dictates of the powerful bishop of Alexandria? If so, why didn't they burn the books instead of hide them? Is it possible that they actually liked these books and decided to hide them away for safekeeping until the tides of scriptural preference shifted and they could be retrieved for posterity in their library of sacred texts? We will never know.

The Nag Hammadi Library and
Early Christian Gnosticism

In *The Da Vinci Code* Leigh Teabing refers to the Gospel of Philip and other books of this collection as "Gnostic Gospels." What does that mean?

Gnosticism is a term that scholars have used for a broad range of religions known from the second and third Christian centuries. It is derived from the Greek word *gnosis*, which means "knowledge." These religions are called Gnostic because they emphasize the need for true knowledge for salvation; more specifically, they require true self-knowledge. It is only when people come truly to

The Gnostic books (*above*) discovered in 1945 near Nag Hammadi, Egypt, and the place where they were found (*left*).

know themselves that they can be delivered from the evils of this world. And, as it turns out, the evils of this world have to do with our material existence itself, for according to Gnostics the world of matter is itself inherently evil and must be escaped by the spirits that are trapped within our (evil, material) bodies. This escape comes by knowing who we really are.

Even though there was a remarkably broad range of belief and practice among different Gnostic groups (just as there are today among groups that call themselves Christian), it appears that most Gnostics in antiquity subscribed to a number of important tenets:

1. *The world*. We have seen that Jewish apocalypticists were dualistic, in that they believed there were two fundamental components of reality: good and evil. Gnostics were even more extreme dualists, believing that the physical world itself is inherently evil, in opposition to the world of the spirit, which is good.

2. *The divine realm*. The true God did not, therefore, create this material world. He is completely spirit. According to the myths that Gnostics told—some of which are preserved among the Nag Hammadi tractates—in eternity past the true God generated other divine offspring who themselves, in pairs, reproduced offspring. But a catastrophe occurred in the divine realm when one of the divine beings (often called Sophia, a feminine deity, whose name means "wisdom") became separated from the rest and spontaneously generated another divine being. The latter, born outside the divine realm, was evil. With his minions who also came into being, he created the material world as a place of imprisonment for the one who had fallen (Sophia).

3. *Humans*. Sophia was thus captured and imprisoned in this material world in the bodies of humans. Many humans have this spark of the divine within them. These people long to escape

this world. Other people don't have the spark within; they are like other animals, who simply cease to exist when they die.

4. *Salvation*. The divine spark within humans can escape only by learning where it came from, how it got here, and how it can return. Deliverance from this evil material world, in other words, comes only by liberating knowledge (gnosis).

5. *The church*. Many Gnostics maintained that Christians who have faith in Christ and do good works can have some modicum of salvation when they die (as opposed to other people, who simply cease to exist). But the real and glorious afterlife will come only to the Gnostics themselves, those who have the divine spark within and who come to the full knowledge of the secrets of salvation.

6. *The divine redeemer*. This knowledge, however, cannot be gained simply by understanding this world. The knowledge must come from outside the world, by a divine redeemer who brings the knowledge of salvation from above. For Christian Gnostics (there were non-Christian Gnostics as well, who had different explanations of salvation), Christ is the one who comes from above to bring this knowledge. Different Gnostics understood Christ in different ways. Some of them were docetists, insisting that Christ, a divine being, came to earth seeming to be a human, but that as a divine being, he was not actually flesh and blood. Other Gnostics believed that Christ was a divine being who came into the body of the man Jesus when he was baptized; while inhabiting Jesus' body, he taught his followers the truth that can bring salvation. He then left Jesus prior to his death. That is why, on the cross, Jesus called out, "My God, my God, why have you forsaken me?" For these Gnostics, the divine element really did abandon Jesus on the cross.

I have been laying out these various tenets not because I think it's important that everyone have a primer on ancient Gnosticism but because in *The Da Vinci Code* Leigh Teabing claims that the so-called Gnostic Gospels of Nag Hammadi portray Christ principally as a human figure, not as divine, in contrast to the Gospels of the New Testament. I hope two things have become clear from this discussion of the Nag Hammadi Library. On one hand, Teabing is right when he maintains that the view of Christ in these Gnostic documents is at odds with what we find in the New Testament. But on the other hand he is absolutely wrong to say that the difference lies in the portrayal of Jesus as uniquely human in these texts. In fact, just the opposite is the case. These texts—including the one Teabing quotes, the Gospel of Philip, as well as others (including one other important to *The Da Vinci Code*, the Gospel of Mary, which was found not at Nag Hammadi but elsewhere)—do not stress the humanity of Christ at all. Some of these texts appear to imagine Christ as a divine being in the likeness of a human. Even more of them understand the man Jesus himself to be human—he is important, however, not as a human but as the temporary residence of the divine Christ, who brings salvation by revealing the truth of the human condition to those capable of learning the knowledge that brings liberation.

Conclusion

In short, Leigh Teabing is right that the discoveries of the Dead Sea Scrolls and the Nag Hammadi Library are important for understanding how the early Christians portrayed Jesus. For critical historians, these documents provide valuable source material for understanding the milieus of Jesus and his early follow-ers in the years after his death. But it is important to know *what* they tell us about those milieus. Misreading or misrepresenting ancient sources is as serious an error as overlooking them alto-gether. And as it turns out, Teabing makes several fundamental mistakes when assessing the importance of these modern ar-chaeological discoveries. The Dead Sea Scrolls are Jewish, not Christian, and are important principally for providing us a sense of the milieu out of which Jesus emerged. They do not actually mention Jesus, however, let alone stress anything about his char-acter. Some of the Nag Hammadi documents, on the other hand, are Christian and do mention Jesus. Included in this collection are noncanonical Gospels that appear to represent a Gnostic perspective. Far from portraying Christ as human, however, these documents are more interested in his divine qualities.

In the next chapter we will examine some of these other Gos-pels themselves, early Gospel texts that did not make it into the New Testament. That examination will reveal further just how far afield Leigh Teabing was in asserting that the Gospels that came to be suppressed in the early church portray Jesus in more human fashion than do the four canonical accounts. Precisely the contrary: it is the Gospels of the New Testament that por-tray Jesus as human, and the other Gospels go much further in portraying him as a superhuman being. This is true not only of the documents found in Nag Hammadi but also of other Gos-pels—Gnostic and otherwise—that have been rediscovered in modern times.

Chapter Three

———————————————

The Other Gospels

As we have seen, one of the key historical issues raised by Leigh Teabing in *The Da Vinci Code* involves an ancient "cover-up." In his view, the early church sought to make the man Jesus into a divine figure. But this proved to be a difficult case for the church to make, since most of the earliest Gospels, Teabing claims, portrayed Jesus as fully human and not divine. The solution to the problem was obvious: the church chose the four Gospels of Matthew, Mark, Luke, and John, which portray Jesus as divine, Teabing asserts, and destroyed all the earlier accounts, which were more historically accurate.

As Teabing explains to Sophie Neveu in his drawing room:

> "Jesus Christ was a historical figure of staggering influence, perhaps the most enigmatic and inspirational leader the world has ever seen. . . . His life was recorded by thousands of followers across the land. . . . More than *eighty* gospels were considered for the New Testament, and yet only a relative few were chosen for inclusion—Matthew, Mark, Luke, and John among them." (p. 231; emphasis in original)

Somewhat later, in Teabing's study, the conversation continues, but it turns to the key question of the relationship of Jesus
and Mary, as portrayed in the Gospels:

> "As I mentioned," Teabing clarified, "the early Church needed
> to convince the world that the mortal prophet Jesus was a *divine*
> being. Therefore, any gospels that described *earthly* aspects of
> Jesus' life had to be omitted from the Bible. Unfortunately for
> the early editors, one particularly troubling earthly theme kept
> recurring in the gospels. Mary Magdalene." He paused. "More
> specifically, her marriage to Jesus Christ." (p. 244; emphases in
> original)

There are several historical errors in Teabing's account. As we
will see in a later chapter, Jesus' words and deeds were by no means
recorded "by thousands" during his lifetime; on the contrary, there
is no evidence that *anyone* recorded the facts of his life while he was
still living. Nor were there eighty Gospels considered for inclusion
in the New Testament. And Matthew, Mark, Luke, and John are
not "among" those that were included in the New Testament—
they were the *only* ones included.

Apart from these factual errors, Teabing's comments raise a
number of interesting historical questions that we can consider:
What other Gospels (outside the New Testament) actually do
exist still today? Do they portray Jesus as human rather than
divine? And do they indicate that he was married to Mary
Magdalene?

In this chapter we will consider several of the other Gospels
that have come down to us. As I've already indicated, Teabing is
wrong to assert that there were eighty other Gospels vying for a
place in the New Testament. The reality is that we don't even
know how many other Gospels were written; we certainly do not

have eighty available to us today, although there are at least a couple of dozen that we know about. Most of these Gospels have become available only in relatively recent times, as they have been discovered accidentally, for example, in the Nag Hammadi Library, uncovered in 1945. One point on which Teabing happens to be correct is that the church did canonize four Gospels and exclude all the others, proscribing their use and (sometimes) destroying them, so that most Christians throughout the history of the church have had access only to the accounts of Jesus recorded in the books of the New Testament. This is not to say, however, that the other Gospels—those outside of the New Testament—are more likely accurate historically, nor is it to say they portray a more human Jesus, who was married to Mary Magdalene. Quite the contrary: as indicated in the previous chapter, most of these other Gospels portray Jesus in even *more* divine terms than do the four in the canon, and in none of the extra-canonical Gospels is there any reference to Jesus having been married, let alone married to his follower Mary Magdalene.

We will be addressing many of these issues in chapters to come. For now we should take a look at a few of our earliest non-canonical Gospels to see how they portray Jesus: as human or as superhuman? I will not try to cover all of our earliest surviving non-canonical Gospels here; these can be found in other places.[1] My intention is simply to give a brief sampling of the kinds of books one can find outside the canon. I will start with one that might be expected to show a very human Jesus, in that it is an account of Jesus as a young boy and the various escapades he was involved with then, as a youth. Unfortunately for Teabing's thesis, even this early account is concerned to portray a super-human Jesus, rather than a human one.

The Infancy Gospel of Thomas

The account called the Infancy Gospel of Thomas (not to be confused with the Coptic Gospel of Thomas discovered near Nag Hammadi) deals with Jesus' life as a young boy.[2] The book is dated by some scholars to the early second century, making it one of the earliest Gospels to have survived from outside the New Testament. The stories in this narrative provide us with entertaining accounts of Jesus' activities beginning at a tender young age. Behind the narrative lies a question that intrigues some Christians even today: "If Jesus was the miracle-working Son of God as an adult, what was he like as a kid?" It turns out that he was more than a little mischievous.

The narrative opens with Jesus as a five-year-old, playing by a stream on the day of the Sabbath. He gathers together some of the muddy water by making a small dam, and then orders the water to be purified—and immediately it is pure. Jesus then makes some clay sparrows by the shore of the stream. But a Jewish man passes by and sees what he has done—he has made something and thereby broken the law of the Sabbath (not to work). The man runs off to tell Joseph, his father. Joseph comes and upbraids Jesus for profaning the Sabbath. But instead of apologizing or repenting for committing a sin, the child Jesus claps his hands and tells the sparrows to be gone. They come to life and fly off chirping— thereby destroying any evidence of malfeasance (Inf. Thom. 2). Jesus, already as a young child, is the author of life and is not bound to human rules and regulations.

One might have expected that with his supernatural powers, Jesus would have been a useful and entertaining playmate for the other kids in town. As it turns out, however, the boy has a temper and is not to be crossed. A child he is playing with decides to take the branch of a willow tree to scatter the pure water Jesus has gathered together. This aggravates the young Jesus, who cries out, "You unrighteous, irreverent idiot! What did the pools of water do to harm you? See, now you also will be withered like a tree, and you will never bear leaves or root or fruit." And Jesus' word is good as gold: "Immediately that child was completely withered" (Inf. Thom. 3:1–3). Jesus goes back home, but "the parents of the withered child carried him away, mourning his lost youth." They then go to Joseph to protest: "What kind of child do you have who does such things?" (Inf. Thom. 3:3). The answer is clear to the reader: Joseph has a supernatural child, one who hasn't learned yet to control his anger.

This is seen again in the next account: when another child accidentally runs into him on the street, Jesus turns in anger and declares, "You shall go no further on your way." The child falls down dead (Inf. Thom. 4:1). (Jesus later raises him from the dead, along with others that he has cursed on one occasion or another.) And Jesus' wrath is not reserved only for other children. Joseph sends him to school to learn to read, but Jesus refuses to recite the alphabet. His teacher pleads with him to cooperate, until Jesus replies with a scornful challenge, "If you really are a teacher and know the letters well, tell me the power of Alpha and I'll tell you the power of Beta." More than a little perturbed, the teacher cuffs the boy on the head, the single largest mistake of an illustrious teaching career. Jesus withers him on the spot. Joseph is stricken with grief and gives an urgent order to Jesus' mother: "Do not let him go outside: anyone who makes him angry dies" (Inf. Thom. 14:1–3).

At one point of the narrative Jesus' reputation causes him to be blamed whenever anything goes wrong. He is playing on a roof with a group of kids, and one of them, a boy named Zenon, accidentally trips, falls off the roof, and dies. The other kids are frightened and run off; Jesus, though, goes to the side of the roof to look down. Zenon's parents arrive at the scene, and what are they to think? There is their child, dead on the ground, and Jesus standing on the roof above him. This supernaturally gifted child has been up to his tricks again, they think. They accuse Jesus of killing their child, but this time he is innocent! And so he jumps off the roof, lands by the child, and speaks to him: "Zenon! Rise up and tell me: did I throw you down?" The boy rises from the dead and says, "Not at all, Lord! You did not throw me down, but you have raised me up!" (Inf. Thom. 9:1–3).

As time goes on, Jesus begins using his powers for good. He saves his brother from a deadly snakebite, he heals the sick, he restores to health and life everyone that he has previously withered or killed. And he proves to be remarkably handy around the house and carpenter shop: when Joseph miscuts a board and is in danger of losing an important customer, Jesus is there to correct his mistakes miraculously. The account concludes with Jesus as a twelve-year-old in the Temple, surrounded by scribes and Pharisees, a narrative familiar to readers of the New Testament, as it has been drawn from chapter 2 of Luke.

As intriguing as this Gospel is, it clearly does not represent an attempt by an early Christian to give what we might think of as a historically accurate account of the young Jesus' life. It is difficult to know whether the stories here were meant to be taken literally as things that happened to the young Jesus, or whether instead they were entertaining flights of the imagination. In either case, the Jesus portrayed here is not merely human; he is a superhuman wunderkind.

The Gospel of Peter

A very different narrative, called the Gospel of Peter, deals not with the young Jesus' life but with his last hours. We do not have the complete text of this Gospel, but only a fragment of it, which was discovered in 1886 in the tomb of an eighth-century Christian monk, buried in upper Egypt. The fragmentary account is very ancient, however, dating back probably to the early second century, making the Gospel of Peter one of the earliest surviving accounts of Jesus' life (actually, of his death and resurrection) from outside the New Testament. Once again, one might expect to find a very human Jesus in this account, but instead it stresses even more his superhuman qualities.[3]

The Gospel fragment as we have it begins with the following words: "but none of the Jews washed his hands, nor did Herod or any of his judges. Since they did not wish to wash, Pilate stood up." This is a significant beginning for two reasons. It shows that just before the fragment begins, the Gospel contained an account of Pilate washing his hands—a story found, among our New Testament Gospels, only in Matthew. And it displays a marked difference from the account in Matthew, which says not a word about anyone *refusing* to wash their hands. Here Herod, the "king of the Jews," and his Jewish judges (unlike the Roman governor, Pilate) refuse to declare themselves innocent of Jesus' blood. This intimates an important aspect of the rest of the account, in that here it is the Jews, rather than the Romans, who are responsible for Jesus' death. This fragmentary Gospel is far more virulently anti-Jewish than any of those that made it into the New Testament.

The narrative continues with the request of Joseph (of Arimathea) for Jesus' body, the mockery of Jesus, and his crucifixion. These accounts are both like and unlike what we read in the canonical

Gospels. For example, in v. 10, Jesus is said to be crucified between two criminals, as in the other Gospels; but then we find the
unusual statement that "he was silent, as if he had no pain." This
last statement could well be taken in a docetic way—perhaps Jesus
appeared to have no pain because he did *not* have any. Another
key verse comes when Jesus is about to die; he utters his "cry of
dereliction" in words similar to, but not identical with, those found
in Mark's account: "My power, O power, you have left me" (v. 19;
cf. Mark 15:34); he is then said to be "taken up," even though his
body remains on the cross. Is Jesus here bemoaning the departure
of the divine Christ from him prior to his death, the view, as we
have seen, of some Gnostic Christians?

After Jesus dies, the account continues by describing his burial
and then, in the first person, the distress of the disciples: "we
fasted and sat mourning and weeping, night and day, until the
Sabbath" (v. 27). As in Matthew's Gospel, the Jewish leaders ask
Pilate for soldiers to guard the tomb. This Gospel, however,
provides more elaborate detail. The centurion in charge is named
Petronius, who, along with a number of soldiers, rolls a huge
stone in front of the tomb and seals it with seven seals. They
then pitch their tent and stand guard.

Then comes perhaps the most striking passage of the narrative, an actual account of Jesus' resurrection and emergence from
the tomb—an account found in none of our other early Gospels.
A crowd has come from Jerusalem and its surrounding neighbor-
hoods to see the tomb. During the night hours, they hear a great
noise and observe the heavens open up; two men descend in great
splendor. The stone before the tomb rolls away of its own accord,
and the two men enter. The soldiers standing guard awaken the
centurion, who comes out to see the incredible spectacle. From
the tomb there emerge three men; the heads of two of them reach

up to the sky. They are supporting the third, whose head reaches up beyond the skies. Behind them emerges a cross. A voice then speaks from heaven: "Have you preached to those who are asleep?" The cross replies, "Yes" (vv. 41–42).

A giant Jesus and a walking, talking cross—this is scarcely a restrained account that focuses on Jesus' human qualities.

The soldiers run to Pilate and tell him all that has happened. The Jewish leaders beg him to keep the story quiet, for fear that they will be stoned once the Jewish people realize what they have done in putting Jesus to death. Pilate commands the soldiers to silence, but only after reminding the Jewish leaders that Jesus' crucifixion was indeed their fault, not his. The next day at dawn, not knowing what has happened, Mary Magdalene goes with several women companions to the tomb to provide a more adequate burial for Jesus' body, but the tomb is empty, save for a heavenly visitor who tells her that the Lord has risen and gone. (This is the one place in the account where Mary is mentioned; there is nothing said otherwise about her having a "special" relationship with Jesus here.) The manuscript then ends in the middle of a story that apparently described Jesus' appearance to some of his disciples (perhaps similar to that found in John 21:1–14): "But I, Simon Peter, and Andrew, my brother, took our nets and went off to the sea; and with us was Levi, the son of Alphaeus, whom the Lord. . ." (v. 60). Here the manuscript breaks off.

This text is called the Gospel of Peter because of this final line: it is written in the first person by someone claiming to be Peter. But it obviously wasn't actually written by Simon Peter, as it appears to have been written in the early second century (hence the heightened anti-Judaism mentioned earlier) long after Peter's death. Still, it is one of our earliest noncanonical accounts of Jesus' last days. Unfortunately for Leigh Teabing's thesis, it does not heighten Jesus' humanity, and it says nothing about Jesus and Mary being intimate, let alone married. Mary is simply the first person (along with her companions) to come to the tomb after Jesus' death—just as she is in the Gospels that made it into the New Testament.

Teabing, of course, does not discuss directly the Infancy Gospel of Thomas or the Gospel of Peter, which were known before the discovery of the Nag Hammadi Library, but he does mention "Gnostic" Gospels uncovered in this find. Do these more recently discovered Gospels bear out his thesis concerning the human Jesus, married to Mary Magdalene?

The Coptic Apocalypse of Peter

One of the most interesting accounts of Jesus' death from the Nag Hammadi Library occurs in a text that is called not a Gospel but an apocalypse (i.e., a revelation of the truth); it is allegedly also by Peter, although it too is pseudonymous. One of the most interesting features of this account is that it is a Gnostic document that was clearly written to *oppose* the kinds of Christians who attacked Gnosticism—that is, those who eventually decided which books to include in the New Testament canon. As it turns out, though, rather than opposing them for thinking that Jesus was divine, it opposes them for maintaining that Jesus was *human*. That is to say, this book runs precisely counter to the claims of Leigh Teabing that the Gnostic Gospels portray a more human, less divine Jesus.

The book begins with the teachings of "The Savior," who informs Peter that there are many false teachers who are "blind and deaf," who blaspheme the truth and teach what is evil.[4] Peter, on the other hand, will be given secret knowledge, that is, gnosis (Apoc. Pet. 73). Jesus goes on to tell Peter that his opponents are "without perception" (i.e., without gnosis). Why? Because "they hold fast to the name of a dead man."[5] In other words, they think that it is Jesus' human death that matters for salvation. For this author, those who maintain such a thing "blaspheme the truth and proclaim evil teaching" (Apoc. Pet. 74).

Indeed, those who confess a dead man cling to death, not to immortal life. These souls are dead and were created for death.

> Not every soul comes from the truth nor from immortality. For every soul of these ages has death assigned to it. Consequently it is always a slave. It is created for its desires and their eternal destruction, for which they exist and in which they exist. They (the souls) love the material creatures which came forth with them. But the immortal souls are not like these, O Peter. But indeed as long as the hour has not yet come, she (the immortal soul) will indeed resemble a mortal one. (Apoc. Pet. 75)

Gnostics in the world, on the other hand, may appear to be like other people, but they are different, not clinging to material things or living according to their desires. Their souls are immortal, even though this is not widely known: "Others do not understand mysteries, although they speak of these things which they do not understand. Nevertheless they will boast that the mystery of the truth is theirs alone" (Apoc. Pet. 76). Who are these who fail to understand, who do not teach the truth? "And there will be others of those who are outside our number who name themselves 'bishop' and also 'deacons,' as if they have received their authority from God. . . . These people are dry canals" (Apoc. Pet. 79).

This is scarcely complimentary to the leaders of the Christian churches: they are not fountains of knowledge and wisdom but dried-up riverbeds.

What, though, is this knowledge that is accessible to the immortal souls, not riveted to material things, misperceived by the ignorant leaders of the church? It is knowledge about the true nature of Christ himself and his crucifixion, which is only mistakenly thought to refer to the human death of Christ for sins. But in fact the true Christ cannot be touched by pain, suffering, and death. He is well beyond them all. What was crucified was not the divine Christ, but simply his physical shell.

In a captivating scene, Peter is said to witness the crucifixion, and admits to being confused by what he sees:

> When he had said those things, I saw him apparently [!] being seized by them. And I said, "What am I seeing, O Lord? Is it you yourself whom they take? . . . Who is this one above the cross, who is glad and laughing? And is it another person whose feet and hands they are hammering?"

Jesus then gives this stunning reply, which shows the true meaning of the crucifixion:

> The Savior said to me, "He whom you see above the cross, glad and laughing, is the living Jesus. But he into whose hands and feet they are driving the nails is his physical part, which is the substitute. They are putting to shame that which is in his likeness. But look at him and me." (Apoc. Pet. 81)

Not Christ himself but only his physical, human likeness is put to death. The living Jesus transcends death—literally transcends the cross—for there he is above it, laughing at those who think they can hurt him, at those who think the divine spirit within him can suffer and die. The spirit of Jesus is beyond pain and death, as are the spirits of those who understand who he really is, who know the truth of who they really are—spirits embodied in a physical likeness, who cannot suffer or die. The vision then continues:

And I saw someone about to approach us who looked like him, even him who was laughing above the cross, and he was filled with a pure spirit, and he was the Savior. . . . And he said to me, "Be strong! For you are the one to whom these mysteries have been given, to know through revelation that he whom they crucified is the firstborn, and the home of demons, and the clay vessel in which they dwell, belonging to Elohim [i.e., the God of this world], and belonging to the cross that is under the law. But he who stands near him is the living Savior, the primal part in him whom they seized. And he has been released. He stands joyfully looking at those who persecuted him. . . . Therefore he laughs at their lack of perception. Indeed, therefore, the suffering one must remain, since the body is the substitute. But that which was released was my incorporeal body." (Apoc. Pet. 82)

The body is just a shell, belonging to the creator of this world [= Elohim; a Hebrew word for God in the Old Testament]. The true self is within and cannot be touched by physical pain. This is true of Jesus and of those among his followers with true knowledge. Those without this true gnosis think they can kill Jesus. The living Jesus, though, rises above it all, laughing them to scorn. And who is really the object of his derision? Those who think that the death of the human Jesus is the key to salvation. An absurd view, a ridiculous view, a laughable view. Salvation doesn't come *in* the body; it comes by *escaping* the body. The dead Jesus does not save; the living Jesus saves. So-called believers who don't understand are not the beneficiaries of Jesus' death; they are mocked by it.

And so this Gospel does not portray Jesus as *more* human than do the Gospels of the New Testament; the real meaning of Jesus completely transcends his humanity. What about other books from the Nag Hammadi Library, including those called Gospels: do they support Leigh Teabing's contention?

The Coptic Gospel of Thomas

Without a doubt, the most famous Gospel from the Nag Hammadi Library is the Coptic Gospel of Thomas (not to be confused with the Infancy Gospel of Thomas, mentioned above). Given its importance, I will spend more time unpacking its message than I have for the other Gospels we have considered.

There have been considerable debates over the Gospel of Thomas since it was first discovered. Among the central issues is the question of whether it is best understood as a "Gnostic" Gospel or not. My own view is that even though the Gospel of Thomas does not lay out the Gnostic system for its readers in clear and coherent fashion, it does *presuppose* a Gnostic system, much as I described it in chapter 2. Jesus, in this Gospel, is the divine revealer of the secret knowledge that can bring liberation from this evil material world. He is portrayed here not as a mere human teacher but as a divine revealer. This portrayal depends on a Gnostic understanding of the world and our place in it.

Before describing the teachings found in the Gospel of Thomas, I should say something about the character of the Gospel as a whole.[6] Unlike the Gospel of Peter, the Gospel of Thomas is a complete text: we have its beginning, its end, and everything in between. It consists of 114 sayings of Jesus and almost nothing else. There are no stories told about Jesus here: no miracles, no travels, no trials, no death, no resurrection, no narrative of any kind. Most of the sayings are simply introduced by the words "Jesus said. . . " followed by another verse that begins the same way. In some instances there is a back-and-forth between Jesus and the disciples, in which they say or ask something and Jesus responds, or he says something and they respond. There is no obvious organizing pattern to the collection of sayings; a few of

The opening of the Coptic Gospel of Thomas, which begins (in the middle of the page) with the words "These are the secret words which the living Jesus spoke, and Didymus Judas Thomas wrote them down."

them hang together by dealing with the same topic or using the same catchwords, but for the most part the sequence appears to be completely random.

Over half of the sayings found in the Gospel of Thomas are similar to sayings found in the New Testament Gospels (79 of the 114, by one count). In some instances, these similarities are quite close. Here, for example, you can find the well-known parable of the mustard seed:

> The disciples said to Jesus, "Tell us what the kingdom of heaven is like." He said to them, "It is like a mustard seed. It is the smallest of all seeds. But when it falls on tilled soil, it produces a great plant and becomes a shelter for birds of the sky." (saying 20; see Mark 4:30–31)[7]

And, in a somewhat terser form than in the New Testament, the comment about the blind leading the blind:

> Jesus said, "If a blind man leads a blind man, they will both fall into a pit." (saying 34; see Matt. 15:14)

But a large number of the sayings do not sound at all like what one finds on the lips of Jesus in the canonical Gospels (except for a few set phrases). Just to take two rather striking instances:

> Jesus said, "This heaven will pass away, and the one above it will pass away. The dead are not alive and the living will not die. In the days when you consumed what is dead, you made it what is alive. When you come to dwell in the light, what will you do? On the day when you were one you became two. But when you become two, what will you do?" (saying 11)

> His disciples said, "When will you become revealed to us and when shall we see you?" Jesus said, "When you disrobe without being ashamed and take up your garments and place them under your feet like little children and tread on them, then will you see the son of the living one, and you will not be afraid." (saying 37)

What is one to make of these peculiar sayings? What do they mean?

We can begin to unravel this Gospel by looking at its striking beginning, which reveals the author's purpose and his understanding of the importance of his collection of sayings and, relatedly, of how one can acquire eternal life:

> These are the secret sayings which the living Jesus spoke and which Didymus Judas Thomas wrote down. And he said, "Whoever finds the interpretation of these sayings will not experience death." (saying 1)

The sayings recorded here are purported to be secret; they are not obvious, self-explanatory, or commonsensical. They are hidden, mysterious, puzzling. Jesus spoke them, and Didymus Judas Thomas wrote them down. And the way to have eternal life is to discover their true meaning.

This is a Gospel that does not stress the importance of Jesus' human death and resurrection for salvation. In fact, the death and resurrection of Jesus are not narrated here, let alone emphasized. Salvation comes not by believing in Christ's passion but by interpreting his sayings.

If understanding these sayings correctly is the prerequisite for eternal life, how are we to interpret them? As I have indicated, in my view (which appears to be that of Leigh Teabing as well) some kind of Gnostic worldview lies behind the Gospel of Thomas. Not that Thomas is trying to advance that worldview, or explicate its mythological bases, or explain its intricacies. But the sayings of this Gospel, on my reading, make the best sense when approached with a sense of the Gnostic milieu within which the author was writing.

For example, saying 1 claims that the one who finds the interpretation of Jesus' secret sayings will not experience death. The sayings are thus secret (not open to the public, but only for those in the know), and their interpretation (*knowing* what they mean) is what brings an escape from the death of this world. Saying 2 is about seeking and finding. Knowledge is to be sought after, and when you realize that everything you thought you knew about this world is wrong, you become troubled. But then you realize the truth about this world and you become amazed. And when that happens, you return, ultimately, to the divine realm from which you came, and rule with the other divine beings over all there is.

Or as expressed in another saying, "Whoever has come to understand the world has found only a corpse, and whoever has found [the] corpse is superior to the world" (saying 56). This material world in fact is dead—no life in it. Life involves the spirit. Once you realize what the world really is—death—you are superior to the world, you rise above it. That's why the one who comes to this realization "will not experience death" (saying 1).

Coming to this realization of the worthlessness of this material world, and then escaping it, is like taking off the clothing of matter (the body) and being liberated from its constraints. Thus an effective image of salvation: "When you disrobe without being ashamed and take up your garments and place them under your feet like little children and tread on them, then will you see the son of the living one and you will not be afraid" (saying 37). Salvation means escaping the body.

According to this Gospel, human spirits originated not in this material world but in the world above:

> Jesus said, "If they say to you, 'Where did you come from?' say to them, 'We came from the light, the place where the light came into being on its own accord. . . .' If they say to you, 'Is it you,' say, 'We are its children, and we are the elect of the living father.'" (saying 50)

Thus we came from the world above, the world of light, where there is no enmity, no division, no darkness; we ourselves came from the one God and are his elect, and he is our ultimate destination:

Jesus said, "Blessed are the solitary and elect, for you will find the kingdom. For you are from it, and to it you will return." (saying 49)

It is indeed amazing that this material world came into being as a place of imprisonment for divine spirits, but as amazing as that is, it would have been completely impossible for things to be the other way around, that human spirits came into being as a result of the creation of matter: "If the flesh came into being because of spirit, it is a wonder. But if spirit came into being because of the body, it is a wonder of wonders. Indeed, I am amazed at how this great wealth [i.e., the spirit] made its home in this poverty [i.e., the material world/body]" (saying 29).

For spirits trapped in this material world it is like being drunk and not being able to think straight, or being blind and not being able to see. Jesus came from above, according to this Gospel, to provide the sobering knowledge or the brilliant insight necessary for salvation, and those who were trapped here were in desperate need of it:

Jesus said, "I took my place in the midst of the world and I appeared to them in flesh. I found all of them intoxicated; I found none of them thirsty. And my soul became afflicted for the sons of men, because they are blind in their hearts and do not have sight. . . . But for the moment they are intoxicated. When they shake off their wine, then they will repent." (saying 28)

Why, then, is it that the "dead are not living and the living will not die" (saying 11)? Because the dead are merely matter, and what is not matter but spirit can never die. How is it that "on the day you were one you became two" (saying 11)? Because you were once a unified spirit, but becoming entrapped in a body, you became two things—a body and a spirit—not one. The spirit must escape, and then it will be one again.

This salvation will not, therefore, be salvation that comes *to* this world; it will be salvation *from* this world. The world itself, this material existence, is not something that was created good (contrary to the doctrines of the orthodox Christians). It is a cosmic catastrophe, and salvation means escaping it. For that reason, the kingdom of God is not something coming to this world, a physical entity that can actually be said to *be* here in this world of matter. It is something spiritual, within:

> If those who lead you say to you, "See the kingdom is in the sky," then the birds of the sky will precede you. If they say to you, "It is in the sea," then the fish will precede you. Rather the kingdom is inside of you, and it is outside of you. . . . When you come to know yourselves . . . you will realize it is you who are the sons of the living Father. (saying 3)

Since this world is a place to escape, no one should be tied to material things: "Do not be concerned from morning until evening and from evening until morning about what you will wear" (saying 36). Instead, all that the world has to offer, all the riches it can provide, should be rejected in order to escape this world: "Whoever finds the world and becomes rich, let him renounce the world" (saying 110). And so one should not be attached to anything in this world, as indicated in the pithiest of the sayings of the Gospel, "Become passers-by" (saying 42). Far from emphasizing human life here and now—or a human Jesus, for that matter—these sayings stress the need to escape from the human trappings of this world.

The key to the salvation brought by Jesus is having the proper knowledge, gnosis—knowledge of who you really are:

> When you come to know yourselves, then you will become known, and you will realize that it is you who are the sons of the

living father. But if you will not know yourselves, you dwell in poverty [i.e., the material world/the body] and you are that poverty. (saying 3b)

Jesus himself is the one who can provide this knowledge, knowledge that the human spirit is divine, as divine as Jesus himself, and in fact one with Jesus: "He who will drink from my mouth will become like me. I myself shall become he, and the things that are hidden will be revealed to him" (saying 108). Jesus is the one who brings the knowledge necessary for the divine spirits to be reunited with the realm whence they came. That is why Jesus is not a "divider" (saying 72) but a unifier.

This stress on becoming one, reunified with the divine realm in which there is no conflict, no division, is why the text emphasizes so strongly oneness, singleness, solidarity: "For many who are first will become last, and they will become one and the same" (saying 4); "Blessed are the solitary and elect, for you will find the kingdom" (saying 22). Or as Jesus indicates when the disciples ask, "Shall we then as children enter the kingdom?":

> When you make the two one, and when you make the inside like the outside and the outside like the inside, and the above like the below, and when you make the male and the female one and the same, so that the male not be male nor the female female; and when you fashion eyes in place of an eye, and a hand in place of a hand, and a foot in place of a foot, and a likeness in place of a likeness, then you will enter the kingdom. (saying 22)

Restoring all things to their original unity, where there are not parts but only a whole, no above and below, no outside and inside, no male and female. That is where there is salvation to those who have been separated off, divided from the divine realm.

Perhaps it is this idea that can make sense of what is possibly the most peculiar and certainly the most controversial part of the

Gospel of Thomas, saying 114, in which Mary Magdalene figures prominently—though certainly not as Jesus' wife and lover:

> Simon Peter said to them, "Let Mary leave us, for women are not worthy of life." Jesus said, "I myself shall lead her in order to make her male, so that she too may become a living spirit resembling you males. For every woman who will make herself male will enter the kingdom of heaven."

The saying has caused a good bit of consternation, especially among feminist historians of early Christianity who are inclined to see, for good reason, that Gnosticism was more open to women and their leadership roles in the church than were the orthodox Christians (see chapter 8 in this volume). But this verse—women (including Mary) must become male in order to enter the kingdom?

It is virtually impossible to understand what the verse can mean without recognizing that in the ancient world, the world of this text, people generally understood gender relations differently from the way we do. Today we tend to think of men and women as two different kinds of the same thing. There are humans, and they are either male or female. In the ancient world genders were not imagined like that. For ancient people, male and female were not two different kinds of human; they were two different *degrees* of human.[8]

As we know from medical writers, philosophers, poets, and others, women in the Greek and Roman worlds were understood to be imperfect men. They were men who had not developed fully. In the womb they did not grow penises. After birth they did not develop fully—did not grow muscular, did not develop facial hair, did not acquire deep voices. Women were quite literally the weaker sex. And in a world permeated with an ideology of power and dominance, that made women subservient and, necessarily, subordinate to men.

All the world, it was believed, operates along a continuum of perfection. Lifeless things are less perfect than living ones; plants are less perfect than animals; animals are less perfect than humans; women are less perfect than men; men are less perfect than the gods. To have salvation, to be united with God, required men to be perfected. But for a woman to be perfected, it meant first passing through the next stage along the continuum and becoming a man.[9] And so salvation for the Gospel of Thomas, which presupposes a unification of all things so that there is no up and down, in and out, male and female, requires that all divine spirits return to their place of origin. But for women to achieve this salvation, they obviously must first become male. The knowledge that Jesus reveals allows for that transformation, so every woman who makes herself male, through understanding his teaching, will enter into the kingdom.

Whereas some Gnostic texts celebrate the divine feminine (as we will see), this one seems to emphasize that the feminine must transcend itself to become masculine. This is scarcely a message Leigh Teabing would have wanted to emphasize!

I should stress that Jesus is portrayed in this text not as a good human teacher but as a divine revealer who himself brings the knowledge necessary for salvation, for both women and men. "When you see one who was not born of a woman [i.e., Jesus, who only appeared to be human], prostrate yourselves on your faces and worship him. That one is your father" (saying 15). Or as he says later in the Gospel, "It is I who am the light which is above them all. It is I who am the call. From me did the all come forth, and unto me did the all extend. Split a piece of wood, and I am there. Lift up the stone, and you will find me there" (saying 77). Jesus is the all in all, who permeates the world and yet comes to the world as the light of the world that can bring the human spirit out of darkness so as to return to its heavenly home by acquiring the self-knowledge necessary for salvation.

Conclusion

In this chapter we have considered just four of our earliest Gospels from outside the New Testament. We will consider a couple of other highly important ones—the Gospels of Philip and Mary—in a later chapter, when we look at the role of Mary Magdalene in the life of Jesus and in the history of the early Church. And of course there were yet other Gospels we have not and will not consider—even though Leigh Teabing is wrong to say that we know of eighty, based on the "thousands" of reports about Jesus from his own lifetime. These other Gospels, however, tend to have been written later than the ones we have considered here, and to be yet more legendary or mythological even than these we have considered. Teabing was right to say that there were lots of Gospels that did not come to be included in the New Testament, and that of all those that were at one time or another considered sacred by one Christian group or another, only four Gospels were eventually allowed into the canon. And he is right to say that the other Gospels were then proscribed from Christian use by the church fathers. But he is wrong to say that if these other Gospels had been included in the New Testament, we would have had a view of Jesus that portrayed him in a more human light. In fact, just the opposite is the case. The extracanonical Gospels tend to portray Jesus as more divine.

How did it happen, then, that the four Gospels of Matthew, Mark, Luke, and John came to be included in the New Testament, but all the others came to be left out? Was this, as Teabing asserts, really the work of the emperor Constantine? This is the question we will be addressing in the next chapter.

Chapter Four

Constantine and the Formation of the New Testament Canon

We have seen that Leigh Teabing was right to say that the four Gospels of the New Testament—Matthew, Mark, Luke, and John—were not the *original* records of Jesus' life or the only Gospels available to the early Christians. Other Gospels were widely available but did not make it into the New Testament—even though Teabing is wrong to state with such assurance that there were "eighty Gospels" that were vying for a place in the canon. But how did the books that came to be included in the New Testament come to be selected? Why is it that only four Gospels were eventually taken to be part of the canon and all the others were left out? How was this process carried out? Who made these decisions? On what grounds? And when?

For Teabing, the answer is clear-cut: it was the fourth-century emperor Constantine who made the decisions. Teabing states this view openly in his conversation with Sophie Neveu in his drawing room:

"More than *eighty* gospels were considered for the New Testament, and yet only a relative few were chosen for inclusion—Matthew, Mark, Luke, and John among them."

"Who chose which gospels to include?" Sophie asked.

"Aha!" Teabing burst in with enthusiasm. "The fundamental irony of Christianity! The Bible, as we know it today, was collated by the pagan Roman emperor Constantine the Great." (p. 231)

As Teabing later states, Constantine needed to create this "new" Bible in order to provide scriptural proof for his view that Jesus was divine rather than human. This led then to the formation of the canon (collection of sacred books) of the New Testament, and to the destruction of all other sacred books that were not chosen to be included:

"To rewrite the history books, Constantine knew he would need a bold stroke. From this sprang the most profound moment in Christian history. . . . Constantine commissioned and financed a new Bible, which omitted those gospels that spoke of Christ's *human* traits and embellished those gospels that made Him godlike. The earlier gospels were outlawed, gathered up, and burned." (p. 234)

Teabing's conspiratorial view of the formation of the canon is intriguing, but for the historian familiar with the actual process of how some books came to be included in the New Testament while others came to be excluded, it is filled with more fiction than fact. The historical reality is that the emperor Constantine had nothing to do with the formation of the canon of scripture: he did not choose which books to include or exclude, and he did not order the destruction of the Gospels that were left out of the canon (there were no imperial book burnings). The formation of the New Testament canon was instead a long and drawn-out process that began centuries before Constantine and did not conclude until long after he was dead. So far as we know, based on our historical record, the emperor was not involved in the process.

In this chapter we will consider that process from beginning to end, in order to see how the canon of Christian scripture actually did come into being, when the process took place, and who was involved in it.

On one point Leigh Teabing's view of the formation of the Christian canon is absolutely right: the canon did not simply appear from heaven soon after Jesus' death. As Teabing puts it in one of his most memorable statements to Sophie Neveu:

> Teabing smiled. ". . . Everything you need to know about the Bible can be summed up by the great canon doctor Martyn Percy." Teabing cleared his throat and declared, "The Bible did not arrive by fax from heaven."
> "I beg your pardon?"
> "The Bible is a product of *man*, my dear. Not of God. The Bible did not fall magically from the clouds." (p. 231)

Rather than just appearing in full and finished form to Christians, the canon was instead the result of a long process, in which Christians sifted through the various books that were written and decided which ones should be included in their sacred canon of scripture and which should be excluded. It was a process that took many years—centuries, actually. It was not (contrary to Teabing's view) the decision of one person, or even just one group of persons (for example, a church council); it was the result of protracted and sometimes rancorous discussion, debate, and disagreement. The process was not concluded until long after Constantine's time, but it started centuries earlier.

The Beginnings of the Process

It may seem strange to us today, but in the ancient world it was unusual for religions to have sacred books that were revered as guides to faith and practice. Apart from Judaism, it appears that none of the religions scattered throughout the Roman Empire used books in this way. That is not to say that religions didn't have beliefs and practices—they did, but these were not rooted in sacred texts that were accepted as divinely given sets of "instructions." Not even the culturally foundational books of Homer—the *Iliad* and the *Odyssey*—were seen this way. They instead were accepted for what they were: a group of very good stories filled with mythological descriptions of the gods. But they were not used as guideposts for what to believe and how to act.

The one exception to the rule that ancient religions lacked sacred books was Judaism. Jews did have a group of books (a canon) that they believed had been given by God, books that described to them who God was, indicated how he had interacted with his people (the Jews) throughout history, guided them on how to worship God, and instructed them in how they were to live together in community. In the days of Jesus, the canon of Jewish scripture (which Christians were eventually to call the Old Testament) was not yet set in stone: different Jews accepted a variety of books as authoritative. But there was wide agreement on the heart of the canon—the Torah (a Hebrew word that means "law" or "guidance"), which consists of what is now the first five books of Jewish scripture: Genesis, Exodus, Leviticus, Numbers, and Deuteronomy. These five books, sometimes called the Pentateuch (which means "five scrolls"), were accepted by all Jews as sacred revelation from God. In these books could be found the stories of how God created the world, how he called the nation of Israel to be his own special people, and how he interacted with the ancestors of the Jewish people, the patriarchs and matriarchs of the faith, including Abraham, Sarah, Isaac, Rebecca, Jacob, Rachel, Moses, and so on. Of even greater significance, these books contained the laws that God had given Moses on Mount Sinai, laws concerning how Jews were to worship God through their sacrifices to him in the Temple and through the observance of certain food laws and festivals (including the Sabbath day), as well as laws that governed their behavior with one another.[1]

Looking back on things, it seems almost inevitable that Christians would eventually have a canon of scripture, because Christianity started out with Jesus, a Jewish teacher who accepted the Jewish Torah, followed its customs, kept its laws, and taught its meaning to his own followers. The earliest Christians, of course, were these followers of Jesus, which means that from the beginning Christians had a sacred canon that they accepted as containing books given by God, the canon of the Jewish scriptures. This made them unusual in the Roman empire—where books for the most part simply did not function this way—but not unique: in having a canon, the Christians were simply following the lead of the Jews.

But Christians were to break off from their Jewish roots, and when they did so, they naturally started collecting sacred texts of their own, which were eventually to be pared down and included in a separate, distinctively Christian canon of scripture, later to be known as the New Testament.[2]

The movement toward a New Testament canon began within the New Testament period itself, that is, during the first Christian century. Here it may be useful to provide some basic dates to make sure we are all on the same chronological page.

Jesus of Nazareth engaged in his public ministry, probably, in the late 20s of the first century CE. He was executed by the Romans probably sometime around 30 CE. The first Christian books were written sometime soon after that. The earliest Christian writings that still survive are those of the apostle Paul, written around 50–60 CE. The Gospels of the New Testament are our earliest surviving accounts of the life of Jesus and were written probably between 70 and 95 CE. The other books of the New Testament were written at about the same time; the last was probably 2 Peter, written possibly as late as 120 CE. And so the New Testament books, as well as some other early Christian literature that did not make it into the New Testament, were written roughly between 50 and 120 CE.

Already within that period it appears that Christians had begun to consider some distinctively Christian authorities to be on a par with the books of the Jewish Bible. Evidence comes in some of the writings of the New Testament itself. To begin with, there are suggestions that Jesus' words and teachings were early on thought of as being as authoritative as the texts of scripture. Jesus himself may have encouraged this understanding by the way he taught. According to some of our earliest accounts, such as the Gospel of Matthew, when Jesus interpreted the Law of Moses, he put his own teachings on a par with the laws Moses gave.[3] Moses, for example, said, "Do not murder." Jesus interprets this to mean "Do not even become angry with another." Moses commanded, "Do not commit adultery." Jesus responds, "Do not even lust after a woman in your heart." Moses instructed, "Do not swear a false oath." Jesus insists, "Do not swear an oath at all!" Jesus' own interpretations were accepted by his followers as being as authoritative as the laws of Moses themselves (see Matt. 5:21–48).

Further evidence of this comes later in the New Testament period. In the book of 1 Timothy, allegedly written by the apostle Paul (many scholars think that it was written pseudonymously, in Paul's name, by a later follower of Paul), the author instructs his Christian readers that they should pay their preacher, and then quotes "scripture" to prove the point (1 Tim. 5:18).[4] What is interesting is that he quotes two passages: one from the Law of Moses and the other from the words of Jesus ("A workman is worthy of his hire"—see Luke 10:7). Here Jesus' words are taken to be on a par with scripture.

So too with the writings of his followers. The last book of the New Testament to be written, as I indicated, was 2 Peter. Interestingly enough, this author (who again appears to be pseudonymous, since Peter himself had died long before it was written) refers to false teachers who misinterpret the "letters of Paul," he says, "just as they do with the rest of the Scriptures" (2 Pet. 3:16). Evidently, then, this unknown Christian author took Paul's letters to be "scripture."

My point is that near the end of the first century and the beginning of the second—hundreds of years before Constantine—Christians were already accepting some books as canonical authority, and choosing which books should be so accepted.

The Motivations for a Collection of Books

What was driving this movement to accept a group of books as canonical authorities? As can be seen from the quotations above, Christians had become accustomed to quoting certain texts in order to establish both what to believe and how to engage in their lives together. Once Jesus had died and was no longer available to give his apostles instructions, there needed to be collections of his teachings for posterity, and once the apostles themselves had begun to die off, their own writings needed to be collected as a repository of true teachings to be followed.

This was especially the case because of the enormous diversity of Christianity, which began to emerge in the first century but was evident with unmistakable clarity in the second century. We think of Christianity in the modern world as extremely diverse, as well we should, given the wildly varying interpretations of the faith represented among those who claim to be followers of Jesus. Just think of the difference between Roman Catholics and Baptists, Greek Orthodox and Mormons, Jehovah's Witnesses and Episcopalians, or New England Presbyterians and Appalachian snake handlers. As significant as the differences among Christian groups are today, however, they pale in comparison with the differences among Christian groups that we know about in the early centuries of the church.

Just in the second century, for example, we know of people who claimed to be following the true teachings of Jesus who believed all sorts of things that would strike most modern-day Christians as bizarre in the extreme. There were, of course, Christians who believed in one God, but others said there were two Gods (the God of the Old Testament and the God of Jesus); yet others said there were 12 gods, or 30 gods, or 365 gods! There were Christians who said the world had been created by the one true God, but others indicated that it had been created by a secondary deity; yet others said it was created by an evil being. There were Christians who maintained that Jesus was both fully human and fully divine; another group, as we have seen, said he was so human he could not be divine; yet others said he was so fully divine he could not be human; others said he was two beings—the human Jesus and the divine Christ. There were Christians who believed that Jesus' death brought about the salvation of the world; others said that Jesus' death had nothing to do with the salvation of the world; still another group said that Jesus never died.

As I pointed out earlier, these different Christian groups—especially the ones holding to the more bizarre of these teachings—could not simply consult their New Testaments in order to see who was right and who was wrong, because there *was* no New Testament. Each of these groups had sacred books that they claimed came from Jesus' own apostles—Gospels, Acts, epistles, apocalypses—and insisted that these books should be accepted as scriptural authority for Christians wanting to know what to believe and how to behave. The battle for scripture really was a battle—a conflict among competing groups of Christians intent on determining the nature of Christianity for all posterity. Only one group won the battle; it was this group that determined what the Christian creed would be like (the creed that emerged from the Council of Nicea) and decided which books would be included in the canon of scripture. Contrary to what Leigh Teabing said, this was not a decision rendered by the emperor Constantine. It was rendered by Christian leaders—those who won the early disputes over Christian belief and practice.[5]

Serapion and the Gospel of Peter

We can get a sense of how the process worked by considering an anecdote told by Eusebius, the "father of church history," whom we met in an earlier chapter. As indicated there, Eusebius wrote a ten-volume history of the Christian church from the days of Jesus down to his own time (the era of Constantine). In this history he recounted many stories about early Christians and their conflicts, including their conflicts over theology and the canon of scripture. One story illuminates the entire process of the formation of the canon of scripture.

In chapter 3 I discussed as one of the earliest surviving Gospels the Gospel of Peter. Prior to the discovery of this Gospel in 1886, we knew of its existence from a passage in Eusebius's *Church History*. Eusebius is telling an account of a once-famous bishop of Antioch named Serapion, who lived in the second half of the second century. Serapion had jurisdiction over churches throughout Syria and occasionally made the rounds to keep tabs on his flock. At one point he visited the church in the village of Rhossus and learned that the Christians there used a Gospel written by Peter in their worship services. Serapion saw no difficulty with that—if Peter the apostle had written a Gospel, then certainly it was acceptable for reading in church. But when he returned to Antioch from his travels, several informers came forward to tell him that the so-called Gospel of Peter contained a false theology. They claimed, in fact, that it was a docetic Gospel, in which Jesus was not portrayed as fully human (see our earlier discussion of docetism).

Once he learned this, Serapion acquired a copy of the book for himself and came to see that in fact there were several passages that could be interpreted in a docetic way. He wrote a little pamphlet "On the So-called Gospel of Peter," and sent it to the Christians of Rhossus with instructions that they were no longer to use the book in their communal services.

This is an interesting tale because it reveals a good deal about how Christians went about deciding whether or not a book should be accepted as part of scripture and suitable for use in church for instruction and guidance. Both the Christians of Rhossus and Serapion agreed that a book that was apostolic—that is, written by one of Jesus' closest followers (or at least a companion of his followers)—was acceptable. But even more, a book had to be "orthodox," that is, it had to represent a correct interpretation of the teaching of Christ. A book that did not do so was obviously not apostolic, since the apostles themselves could be trusted to convey the true meaning of Jesus and his teaching. In Serapion's view, the so-called Gospel of Peter was not orthodox; it therefore could not have been written by Peter. For that reason, it was not to be used as part of the Christian worship services. It was, in other words, to be excluded from the canon.

All of this took place 150 years before Constantine.

Irenaeus and the Fourfold Scripture

But is it true that Constantine was responsible for making the *final* decision about the four Gospels that came to be included in the New Testament, as Leigh Teabing claims? Were there a variety of Gospels still widely accepted in the early fourth century from which Constantine chose four to be included in the final canon of scripture?

Even this is not a historically accurate view. Not only were certain "heretical" texts such as the Gospel of Peter excluded by the majority of Christians in the second century, but the fourfold Gospel canon of Matthew, Mark, Luke, and John was itself established long before Constantine as well.

We are able to trace the beginnings of the fourfold Gospel canon through certain church writers of the second century. One of the most famous authors of the period was a figure known to history as Justin Martyr (*martyr* is a descriptive title, not a name), who was executed as a Christian in the second half of the second century, just about the time Serapion was writing his letter to the

Christians of Rhossus. We are fortunate to have extensive writings from Justin, in which he tries to explain to Christianity's cultured despisers that, contrary to widely held opinion, Christianity was not a threat to the unity of the empire and that Christians were not the notorious violators of social decency that they were sometimes made out to be. Christians, in fact, Justin maintained, represented the one true religion given by the one true God.

In making his case, Justin sometimes quotes from earlier Christian texts, including the Gospels. But he never names these books: he instead simply calls them the "Memoirs of the Apostles." And he never indicates that there were just four of them.

Writing some thirty years later, around 180 CE, was another important Christian author named Irenaeus. The thirty years separating Justin and Irenaeus were significant ones for the history of Christianity, for it was in those years that various Gnostic heresies had begun to flourish (each with its own theology) and the prominent Christian teacher Marcion (denounced by Justin and Irenaeus as an arch-heretic) had spread his teachings far and wide. Marcion insisted that there were two Gods, the God of the Jews and the God of Jesus, who had sent Jesus into the world (as a phantasm: Marcion was a docetist) to save people from the wrathful God of the Jews.[6]

How were opponents of the Gnostics and Marcion (and of other so-called false teachers) to convince their readers about the "truth" of the religion? That is, how were Christian leaders to counteract the theological notions of others and to promote their own views as being those of Jesus and his followers? The easiest way, of course, was to claim support for their views in the books written by Jesus' own apostles. Given the heightened threat by heretical false teachers such as Gnostics and Marcion between the time of Justin and of Irenaeus, it is no surprise to see that

Irenaeus has a much more fixed idea of which books belong in the scriptures. In fact, for Irenaeus, there are only four Gospels—Matthew, Mark, Luke, and John. Anyone who chooses only one of the four Gospels (e.g., Marcion used only Luke; some Gnostics used only John) or anyone who includes any other Gospels (e.g., the Gospel of Peter or the Gospel of Thomas) has gone astray.

How does Irenaeus argue his view? He points out that there are four corners of the earth, over which the four winds blow, carrying the truth of the Christian gospel—which must therefore be built on four pillars, the pillars of Matthew, Mark, Luke, and John. Four corners of the earth, four winds, and four Gospels—what could be more natural?[7]

Canon Lists from Early Christianity

From about the time of Irenaeus comes our first canon list—that is, a list of books that an author (this one is anonymous) believes should be accepted as part of the Christian canon. This list, the Muratorian Canon, is named for the eighteenth-century scholar L. A. Muratori, who discovered it in a library in Milan. The manuscript that contains the list was produced in the eighth century, but the list itself appears to have been originally written in Rome near the end of the second century.[8]

The beginning of the text in the manuscript is regrettably lost. But given the way the fragment itself starts, there can be little doubt about the books it initially described: ". . . at which nevertheless he was present, and so he placed [them in his narrative]. The third book of the Gospel is that according to Luke."[9] The author goes on to describe who Luke was, and then to speak of the "fourth of the Gospels," which "is that of John." This list, in other words, begins by discussing the four Gospels, the third and fourth of which are Luke and John. It is fairly clear that the list began by discussing Matthew and Mark, the latter discussion preserved only in the last part of its final sentence.

So the Muratorian Canon includes the four Gospels that eventually made it into the New Testament, and no others. After discussing John, the canon names the Acts of the Apostles and then the epistles of Paul—mentioning nine epistles to seven churches (Corinthians, Ephesians, Philippians, Colossians, Galatians, Thessalonians, and Romans), two of which (Corinthians and Thessalonians) he wrote to twice, and then four to individuals (Philemon, Titus, and two to Timothy). This canon, in other words, includes all thirteen Pauline epistles. It explicitly rejects, however, the epistle "to the Laodiceans" and the one "to the Alexandrians," both of which were "forged in Paul's name to further the heresy of Marcion." These, it indicates, in a memorable image, "cannot be received into the catholic church, for it is not fitting that gall be mixed with honey." (Note that these books were not to be burned; they simply were not to be *read* or, presumably, copied.)

The canon goes on then to list as acceptable the epistle of Jude, two epistles of John, the *Wisdom of Solomon* (a book that obviously did not make it into the New Testament), the Apocalypse of John, and the Apocalypse of Peter (not to be confused with the Coptic Apocalypse of Peter we discussed in the previous chapter), indicating that some Christians are not willing to have the latter read in church. It maintains that a book called *The Shepherd* of Hermas should be read, but not in church as scripture, since "Hermas wrote [it] very recently, in our times, in the city of Rome, while bishop Pius, his brother, was occupying the [episcopal] chair of the church of the city of Rome" (lines 73–76). In other words, it is a recent production (near to "our times") and is not by an apostle (but by the brother of a recent bishop). Hence it cannot be included in the canon.

The list concludes by indicating other rejected books: "We accept nothing whatever of Arsinous or Valentinus or Miltiades, who also composed a new book of psalms for Marcion, together with Basilides, the Asian founder of the Cataphrygians. . . ." Thus the list ends as it began, in midsentence.

When the totals are added up, this second-century author accepted twenty-two or twenty-three of the twenty-seven books that eventually made it into the New Testament. The excluded ones are Hebrews, James, 1 and 2 Peter, and one of the Johannine epistles (he accepts two of the three that we have, but doesn't indicate which two). In addition, he accepts the *Wisdom of Solomon* and, provisionally, noting some dissent, the Apocalypse of Peter. And finally he rejects some books either because they are heretical—the Marcionite forgeries of Paul's letters to the Alexandrians and the Laodiceans and other forgeries attributed to Gnostics and Montanists—or because they do not meet his criteria for canonicity.

Criteria for Inclusion

What are those criteria? As it turns out, they are the same four criteria that were used across a broad spectrum of authors of the second and third centuries. For a book to be admitted into the canon of scripture, it had to be:

1. *Ancient.* A sacred authority had to date back to near the time of Jesus. And so *The Shepherd* of Hermas could not pass muster since it was, relatively speaking, a recent production.

2. *Apostolic.* An authority had to be written by an apostle—or at least by a companion of the apostles. And so the Muratorian Canon accepts the Gospels of Luke (written by Paul's companion) and John and the writings of Paul. But it rejects the forgeries in Paul's name by the Marcionites. We saw a similar criterion in the case of the Gospel of Peter: initially it was accepted by the Christians of Rhossus because of its apostolic pedigree; once it was decided Peter could not have written it, though, it was ruled out of court.

3. *Catholic.* Books had to have widespread acceptance among established churches to be accepted into the canon. In other words, they had to be "catholic," the Greek term for "universal." Hence the waffling in the Muratorian Canon over the status of the Apocalypse of Peter.

4. *Orthodox.* Far and away the most important criterion, though, had to do with the nature of the views set forth in a book. To some extent, in fact, the other criteria were handmaidens to this one. For if a book was not orthodox, it was obviously not apostolic ("obviously," that is, to the one making the judgment), ancient (it must have been forged recently), or catholic (in that none of the other orthodox churches would have had anything to do with it). Hence Serapion on the Gospel of Peter. How did he *know* that Peter hadn't written it? Because it contained something that looked like a docetic Christology, and obviously Peter could not have written such a thing.

Eusebius and the Canon in the Early Fourth Century

The debates raged on in Christian circles concerning the precise contour of the New Testament scriptures for a long time after the creation of the Muratorian canon in the late second century. Still, despite the claims of Leigh Teabing, almost everyone in the orthodox church agreed that the four Gospels, the Acts, the thirteen Pauline epistles, 1 Peter, and 1 John should be included. But there were extensive disagreements about others.

That the issues were not resolved even by the time of Constantine is evident from the writings of the early-fourth-century "father of church history" himself, Eusebius, who at one point in his *Church History* opts to discuss the canon and shows beyond any doubt that the issues were by no means resolved even a century and a half after the Muratorian Canon.[10]

Eusebius's stated intention is "to summarize the writings of the New Testament" (*Church History* 3.25.1). But it proves to be a complicated matter, since as Eusebius indicates, many of the important issues continued to be debated. And so he sets out four categories of books. The first he calls "acknowledged" books—meaning those books accepted by all sides within the orthodox tradition (the only one he is concerned with at this point): the four Gospels, the Acts, the epistles of Paul (among which he includes Hebrews), 1 John and 1 Peter, and "if it really seems right," he says, the Apocalypse of John. Clearly, even the acknowledged books are not universally acknowledged, as he goes on to comment on the Apocalypse: "concerning which we shall give the different opinions at the proper time."

His second category involves books that are "disputed," meaning that they may well be considered canonical, but their status is debated by some. Included in this group are James, Jude, 2 Peter, and 2 and 3 John.

Eusebius then names books he considers "spurious," a word that typically means "forged" but which in this context appears to mean "inauthentic, though sometimes considered canonical."

These include such books as the Acts of Paul, *The Shepherd* of Hermas, the Apocalypse of Peter, the Epistle of Barnabas, the Didache of the Apostles, and the Gospel According to the Hebrews. Somewhat oddly, Eusebius also includes in this group, "if it seems right," the Apocalypse of John—odd because one might expect this to be listed as "disputed" rather than "spurious."

Finally, Eusebius provides a list of books that are heretical and not to be accepted in the church: the Gospels of Peter, Thomas, and Matthias, and the Acts of Andrew and John.

Constantine's Requisition of Fifty Christian Bibles

So the canon was not finalized even by Constantine's day, even though it was agreed among all "orthodox" Christians that the four Gospels of Matthew, Mark, Luke, and John were canonical scripture. Constantine had nothing to do with that decision.

There is only one hint from any ancient source, in fact, that Constantine played any role at all in the formation of the Christian canon, and it may be this that Leigh Teabing alludes to in his comments to Sophie Neveu when he says that "Constantine commissioned and financed a new Bible, which omitted those gospels that spoke of Christ's *human* traits" (p. 234).

In his *Life of Constantine* Eusebius tells us that in the year 331 the emperor made a request of Eusebius personally for fifty manuscripts of the Christian Bible to be produced for churches that he was having built in his imperial city, Constantinople. These books were "to be written on fine parchment in a legible manner, and in a convenient portable form, by professional scribes thoroughly accomplished in their art."[11] Eusebius com-

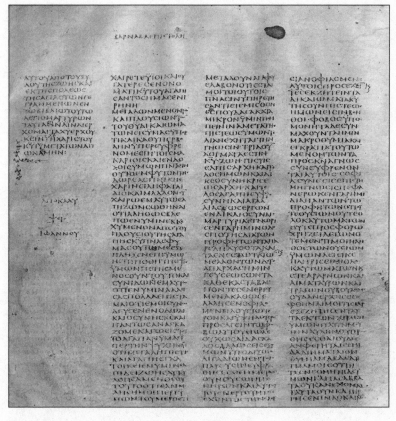

The Codex Sinaiticus, the oldest surviving manuscript of the entire New Testament. This fourth-century manuscript includes *The Shepherd* of Hermas and the Epistle of Barnabas (the first page of which is pictured here), books that were considered part of the New Testament by some Christians for several centuries.

ments that once he received this order of Bibles, he immediately executed it—evidently using the scriptorium (scribal copying room) at his home church of Caesarea as the place where the copies of these scriptures were made.

This order for Bibles did not involve any decision on Constantine's part concerning which Gospels were to be excluded (those that stressed Jesus' humanity) or which included (those stressing only his divinity), and there is nothing to indicate, contrary to Teabing's claim, that it led to the burning of other Gospels. Constantine needed some Bibles for his churches, and he ordered them from Eusebius, whose home church was well equipped to provide them. Their contents were not a matter of concern, as both Constantine and Eusebius evidently knew which books would be appropriately included in these Bibles: certainly at least the four Gospels that were everywhere accepted already by orthodox Christians, and possibly other books as well. As it turns out, we have two magnificent biblical manuscripts that survive from just this period, called the Codex Sinaiticus and Codex Vaticanus. Some scholars have thought that these were two of the copies that Eusebius had prepared in execution of Constantine's request.

Conclusion: The Closing of the Canon

As we have seen, Leigh Teabing was right to insist that "the Bible did not arrive by fax from heaven." The New Testament came into being over a long period of time and as the result of many and protracted disagreements among Christians concerning which books to include and which to exclude. Teabing is wrong to think, however, that Constantine had anything to do with the matter—

or indeed that any single figure, even an emperor, could "rewrite" the Christian Bible overnight. The formation of the canon started centuries before Constantine, and the establishment of the four-fold Gospel canon of Matthew, Mark, Luke, and John was virtually in place 150 years before his day.

On the other hand, it is equally striking that even during Constantine's day the matter was not brought to final resolution— not by him and not by the Council of Nicea, which he called (and which in fact did not deal with the matter of canon). This can be seen by the circumstance that not even Eusebius had a closed canon of scripture: the status of some books was still up for grabs. And so they would be for decades yet to come.

It comes as a shock to some people to learn that our twenty-seven-book canon was not decided for three hundred years or more after the books of the New Testament themselves had been written. In fact, the first time that anyone we know of listed our books as *the* books of the New Testament (these twenty-seven and no others) came nearer to the end of the fourth century, some fifty years after Constantine's death. In an earlier chapter we met Athanasius, who as a young man was an important voice at the Council of Nicea. He was later to become bishop of Alexandria and a powerful figure in worldwide Christendom. Every year, as bishop, he wrote a letter to the churches of Egypt under his jurisdiction, in which he set for them the date for the celebration of Easter (this was before calendars indicated such things years in advance) and provided them with whatever pastoral advice he considered appropriate. In his thirty-ninth such letter, written in 367 CE, Athanasius included among his advice a list of books that he felt were appropriate to be read in church as the canonical scriptures. He listed our twenty-seven books of the

New Testament, neither more nor less. This marked the beginning of the end of the formation of the canon of the Christian Bible. There continued to be debates about the matter for some decades, but eventually most Christians ended up agreeing with the canon laid out by Athanasius, so that in some sense it was he who provided the authoritative statement concerning which books would and which books would not form the canon of New Testament scripture.

Part Two

Jesus and Mary Magdalene

Chapter Five

The Historical Sources for Jesus

As we have seen, at the outset of *The Da Vinci Code*, Dan Brown states as a "fact" that "all descriptions of artwork, architecture, documents, and secret rituals in this novel are accurate" (p. 1). My concern in this book is not with the artwork, architecture, or secret rituals, but with the documents that Brown describes. The problem is that most of his readers will have no grounds on which to evaluate what he says, for example, about the other Gospels that are not found in the New Testament, or the formation of the canon of scripture, or the role of Constantine in shaping the Christian Bible. And so I have thought it important to set the record straight, insofar as possible, and to engage in critical history so as to separate the historical fact from the literary fiction. As it turns out, much of what Brown sets forth about the early Christian documents, largely on the lips of his Grail expert Leigh Teabing, is built into the fabric of his fictional narrative and cannot be trusted as part of the historical record.

Nowhere is that more true than in his description of the surviving sources for understanding the historical Jesus. As we will see in a later chapter, numerous statements about what Jesus was really like and what he really did—most notably, that he married and had sex with Mary Magdalene, producing a child—form the historical backdrop of the novel. Without these historical claims, the narrative would lose its very foundation. These statements about Jesus are supposedly based on documentary evidence. The basic argument of the novel is that the four Gospels of the New Testament cannot be trusted to provide a historically accurate account of Jesus' life but that there are in existence other accounts that *are* reliable. These exist because of the thousands of reports of Jesus' life made in his own day. As Leigh Teabing says in his conversation with Sophie Neveu:

> Jesus Christ was a historical figure of staggering influence, perhaps the most enigmatic and inspirational leader the world has ever seen. . . . His life was recorded by thousands of followers across the land. . . . More than *eighty* gospels were considered for the New Testament, and yet only a relative few were chosen for inclusion—Matthew, Mark, Luke, and John among them." (p. 231)

We have already seen that the latter claim—that there were at least eighty Gospels vying for a spot in the Christian Bible—is not correct. What about the former? What has happened to these thousands of reports of Jesus produced during his lifetime? Teabing later claims that they were shunted to one side and then destroyed when Constantine formed the canon of the New Testament:

> "Because Constantine upgraded Jesus' status almost four centuries *after* Jesus' death, thousands of documents already existed chronicling His life as a *mortal* man. To rewrite the history books, Constantine knew he would need a bold stroke. From this sprang the most profound moment in Christian history. . . . Constantine commissioned and financed a new Bible, which omitted those gospels that spoke of Christ's *human* traits and embellished those

gospels that made Him godlike. The earlier gospels were outlawed, gathered up, and burned." (p. 234)

But as it turns out, Teabing claims, not all of these earlier
documents were destroyed. The mysterious sect known as the
Priory of Sion has kept thousands of these records safe over the
centuries, along with the remains of Mary Magdalene. These
thousands of documents have been stored in "four enormous
trunks" and are called the "Purist Documents." As Teabing later
explains to Sophie, this treasure trove includes

> "thousands of pages of unaltered, pre-Constantine documents,
> written by the early followers of Jesus, revering Him as a wholly
> human teacher and prophet. Also rumored to be part of the trea-
> sure is the legendary 'Q' *Document*—a manuscript that even the
> Vatican admits they believe exists. Allegedly it is a book of Jesus'
> teachings, possibly written in His own hand."

Sophie is incredulous, and asks:

> "Writings by Christ Himself?"
> "Of course," Teabing said. "Why wouldn't Jesus have kept a
> chronicle of His ministry? Most people did in those days." (p. 256)

Notwithstanding Dan Brown's claim to present a factual account of the documents in his narrative, here again we are dealing with fiction instead of historical truth. I can point out the
following concerning the most obvious fictional claims: (1) It's
not true that thousands of Jesus' followers wrote accounts of his
life during his lifetime. So far as we know, no one did. Almost all
his followers were most likely illiterate. (2) Nor did most people
in his time keep a chronicle of their own lives. Most people could
not even write. (3) Relatedly, there is no shred of evidence to

suggest that Jesus himself kept a record of his ministry. On the contrary, so far as we know, Jesus never wrote anything. (4) The Q document is not a source written by Jesus; it is a hypothetical document that scholars believe once contained sayings of Jesus, written about twenty years after his death, and used as a source for their Gospels by Matthew and Luke (as we will see later).

I should stress that I am not objecting to Dan Brown's inventing claims about early Christian documents as part of his fictional narrative; the problem is that he indicates that his accounting of early Christian documents is historically accurate, and readers who don't know the history of early Christianity will naturally take him at his word. But there is more fiction than fact, not just in the plot of *The Da Vinci Code* but also in its discussion of the early documentary record about Jesus.

In the next chapter we will see what we can actually know about Jesus himself—what he said and did (for example, whether he was married, and whether he had sex with Mary Magdalene and had a child with her). In this chapter I'm more interested in the sources of our knowledge about such things. Were there accounts of Jesus' life written from his own time? Are there sources outside the New Testament that can help us know about the facts of his life? Are the documents found inside the New Testament of any use for us in this quest for information about the historical Jesus? Are the New Testament Gospels, for example, historical records—or are they too merely fictional narratives? It may be useful for us to begin by explaining what we do *not* have as sources for the life of the historical Jesus, and then to consider sources that are still available to us and to see how we can read these sources critically in order to establish the most plausible historical narrative.

Our Need of Sources

The first thing I need to stress is a point that I made in the introduction: anyone who says anything about Jesus (or about anybody
else from the past) has to have a source of information. This should
seem obvious, but maybe it's not so obvious to everyone, for there
are lots of people who say lots of things about Jesus all the time—
preachers, televangelists, historians, theologians, Sunday school
teachers, Mormon missionaries, even the guy next door. How does
everyone seem to know so much—or to have so many opinions—
about who Jesus was? The reality is that people can't know *anything* about Jesus unless they have learned it from a source. Or
rather, there are two options (this, again, is true of everything
from the past): either they have learned something from a source
or they have made it up themselves.

The problem, of course, is that most people don't have ancient historical sources for their claims about Jesus. Most people
have learned what they know, or what they think they know,
from other people (for example, a minister or a talking head on
a TV program). But where did *these* people get there information? Usually from other people. And where did *they* get their
information. From others. And so it goes.

Ultimately, everything goes back either to a historical source
or to someone who made things up. Even historical sources,
though, were written by people. Where did the authors of these
historical sources get their information? Same options—either
from others or from their own imaginations. The mere fact that
a source is ancient doesn't necessarily make it reliable; it simply
makes it older than sources today. No one who thinks about this
at any length really doubts it—it's just that many people have
never thought about it. For we know beyond a reasonable doubt

that even ancient sources, close to Jesus' day, sometimes made up information (or relied on others who made it up). Otherwise all the stories we have already discussed in chapter 3 would be historically accurate—that Jesus really did go around zapping his playmates when he was five years old, as in the Infancy Gospel of Thomas, or really did emerge from his tomb as tall as a skyscraper with a walking, talking cross following him, as in the Gospel of Peter. But everyone recognizes these accounts as fictions. Which means these are stories that someone made up.

Since all the stories about Jesus ultimately go back to one source or another, the question naturally arises of which sources are historically reliable. Are there sources that give actual historical information instead of fictional flights of fancy? And how do we know which sources can be trusted as historical? These are questions that historians wrestle with as they try to establish the facts of Jesus' life. These facts cannot be based on mere hearsay or historical imagination. They have to be based on reliable sources. But what sources are there, and how can we extract historical information from them?

As we will see in a moment, the oldest and best sources we have for knowing about the life of Jesus—despite what Leigh Teabing intimates—are the four Gospels of the New Testament, Matthew, Mark, Luke, and John. This is not simply the view of Christian historians who have a high opinion of the New Testament and its historical worth; it is the view of all serious historians of antiquity of every kind, from committed evangelical Christians to hardcore atheists. This view is not, in other words, a biased perspective of only a few naive wishful thinkers; it is the conclusion that has been reached by every one of the hundreds (thousands, even) of scholars who work on the problem of establishing what really happened in the life of the historical Jesus, scholars who (unlike Teabing and his inventor, Dan Brown) have learned Greek and Hebrew, the languages of the Bible, along with other related languages such as Latin, Syriac, and Coptic, scholars who read the ancient sources in the ancient languages and know them inside and out. We may wish there were other, more reliable sources, but ultimately it is the sources found within the canon that provide us with the most, and best, information. I do not mean to say that these sources are unproblematic. In fact, they are riddled with problems, as we will see. But when used judiciously, they can yield important information about what Jesus really said and did.

Before we consider these accounts of Jesus' life, though, what can we say about the other surviving sources, those outside the canon of the New Testament?

Noncanonical Sources

Unfortunately, as I've indicated, we don't have a single word from Jesus' own hand. And contrary to the claims of Leigh Teabing, we don't have thousands of documents written by his contemporaries about him. We don't even have hundreds, or even dozens. In fact, we don't have *any* document written by a single eyewitness to the life of Jesus. This may seem counterintuitive: surely someone who was so significant—someone who had so many followers and allies and enemies, someone who did such spectacular deeds and delivered such spectacular teachings, someone who inspired a great world religion with many millions of followers throughout the course of history—must have been the talk of the Roman Empire. Surely people wrote about him. Surely we have *something* from his own day!

But no, unfortunately, we have nothing. No account from a disciple (we'll look at the New Testament Gospels in a moment), no account from an enemy among the Pharisees or the Sadducees, nothing among the Dead Sea Scrolls, nothing by any Roman citizen or imperial authority. There are no birth records, no accounts of his miracles, no transcripts of his trial, no record of his death written at the time. All our sources are later.

It is conventional to divide these (later) noncanonical sources for Jesus' life into those that are pagan (meaning by an author who was Greek or Roman or anything else other than Jewish or Christian), those that are Jewish, and those that are Christian.

Pagan Sources

It comes as a surprise to most people to learn that among our pagan sources there is nothing that can help us know what Jesus said and did. As I indicated, Jesus' ministry took place in the 20s of the first century. Suppose we limit our inquiry to the entire first century—the thirty years or so of Jesus' life and the seventy years afterward. What pagan sources survive that can tell us something about him? As it turns out, there is not a solitary pagan source from this period that says *anything* about him. This is not to say that we have no pagan writings from the first century. On the contrary, we have numerous examples—writings of historians, experts on religion, philosophers, poets, administrators, and natural scientists; personal letters (hundreds of them); and inscriptions set up in public places. In none of these vast resources is there any discussion of Jesus. In fact, his name is never even mentioned by a pagan source of the first century at all.

The first reference to Jesus in a pagan source does not come until the year 112 CE, in the writings of a governor of a Roman province, whose name was Pliny.[1] In a letter he wrote to the

Roman emperor Trajan, Pliny indicates that there were "Christians" in his province who were illegally gathering together to "worship Christ as a god." That's all he says about Jesus himself. It's our first reference to him in a pagan source, and it occurs eighty years after his death. A few years later Jesus is mentioned by the Roman historian Tacitus, who does indicate a couple of things about him—namely, that he lived in Judea, where he was crucified as a troublemaker by the Roman procurator Pontius Pilate (who governed Judea from 26 to 36 CE) during the reign of the emperor Tiberius.

If we limit our search to the first hundred years after Jesus' life, these are the only certain references to him among our pagan sources. There's obviously not much to go on here if we want to know what Jesus really said and did.

Jewish Sources

You might expect to find Jesus discussed more frequently in non-Christian Jewish sources of the first century, since he was, after all, a Jew. Unfortunately, there is not much here either. There are not nearly as many Jewish sources from the period as pagan ones, of course, but there are some, including the writings of the prolific Jewish philosopher Philo of Alexandria and of the Jewish historian Flavius Josephus. Philo never mentions Jesus; nor does any other Jewish source of the time, except Josephus. Josephus was the author of a number of works, several of which still survive today, including a twenty-volume history of the Jews from the very beginning (Adam and Eve) up to his own day, near the end of the first century (he wrote this account in 93 CE). In this history he discusses a very large number of important Jewish figures, including several from near his own time (including some others named Jesus). And as it turns out, he does mention Jesus of Nazareth twice. In one reference he discusses a man named James, who was the "brother of Jesus, who is called the messiah." That's all he says about him in this reference. In the other reference, however, he gives fuller information: that Jesus was known to be a doer of "spectacular deeds," that he had followers among both Greeks and Jews, that he was delivered over to Pontius Pilate by the "leaders" of the Jewish people, that he was crucified, and that his followers continued down to Josephus's own day.[2] Unfortunately, Josephus provides no other information about Jesus' life.

From within a hundred years of Jesus' death, this is all we have from non-Christian sources. So if we want to know more about what Jesus really said and did, we are necessarily limited to the Christian sources.

Christian Sources

As we have seen, Leigh Teabing insists that there were thousands of such sources from Jesus' own day. If there ever were such sources, none of them survives. But there are solid historical reasons for thinking that such sources never did exist.

It is important to reflect for a minute on the nature of Jesus' following, so far as we can know about it from the few sources that do happen to be available to us. Jesus was from rural Galilee. His followers were peasants of the Jewish lower classes there, for the most part—farm workers, probably (notice all his parables about seeds, plants, trees, and harvests), fishermen, and the like. Did these people write accounts of his life? The problem is that ancient historians have come to realize that the vast bulk of the population of Jesus' day was illiterate, able neither to read nor to write. It is difficult to establish literacy levels in antiquity, but the most reliable modern study, by Columbia University professor William Harris, indicates that at the very best of times in the ancient world (for example, in Athens during the fifth century BCE, the time of Socrates and Plato), only 10–15 percent of the populace was even functionally literate (able to read and perhaps sign simple documents such as contracts).[3] High literacy rates, such as we now experience in the modern West, were unheard of in antiquity, when it never would have occurred to governmental (or private) agencies to devote the massive resources required to ensuring that everyone could read and write (widespread literacy came about only with the industrial revolution). This means that at the best of times 85–90 percent of a population was illiterate. Those who were able to read and possibly write (the latter requires more extensive training) were the upper classes with the resources and leisure to educate their children. Literacy rates were much lower in an area such as rural Galilee, where most people were subsistence farmers, fishermen, or artisans, who had no need to learn their letters.[4]

And so what about Jesus' followers? The only explicit reference to their literacy comes in the book of Acts, which indicates that two of the chief disciples, Peter and John, were in fact illiterate (Acts 4:13). What about the others? There's little reason to think the story was any different for them. And so not only do we not have the alleged thousands of reports from Jesus' own day written by his followers, but there are compelling reasons to think that there never were these thousands of reports, or even hundreds, or dozens, or . . . any.

The accounts that we do have are all from later writers. Strikingly, these writers do not appear to have been among Jesus' own immediate followers. Take the four Gospels of the New Testament, which we will examine at greater length momentarily. These are written in Greek, by highly educated and well trained authors, some thirty to sixty years after Jesus' death. Jesus' followers, however, were Aramaic-speaking peasants from Galilee who evidently did not speak Greek, let alone know how to compose lengthy accounts (or even to read) in Greek. The Gospels of the New Testament were apparently written not by his closest followers in his own day but decades later by more highly educated Christians who based their narratives on oral traditions that had been in circulation in the intervening years since his death.[5]

But before turning to these Gospels, what other Christian sources exist from outside the New Testament?

The most important ones are the other Gospels, including those we have already discussed, the relatively early reports of such texts as the Infancy Gospel of Thomas, the Gospel of Peter, the Coptic Gospel of Thomas, and so on. And when I say "relatively" early, I mean that these were written within about two hundred years of Jesus' death. They are not contemporary accounts, or even close to it. They appeared many decades, possibly a century or more, after Jesus died. Moreover, as we have seen, these accounts are highly legendary, not the kind of historical record that we would like to have in deciding what Jesus was really like and determining what he actually said and did. This applies as well to the documents we will be considering in a later chapter, the Gospels of Philip and Mary, which do mention Jesus' relationship with Mary Magdalene, but which were also later works of the second (or third) century, not accounts written in Jesus' own day (or even close to it) by people who were there as eyewitnesses to the events of his life.

Historians, therefore, who want to know about the life of Jesus are restricted for the most part by the nature of our sources to those that occur within the canon, with the possible addition of several noncanonical accounts such as the Gospels of Thomas and Peter. We will see in the next chapter how these sources can be used to establish what Jesus really said and did. Before moving there, however, we should say some more things about the sources that occur within the canon of scripture.

Canonical Sources

One might naturally wonder if other books of the New Testament could be used to establish the facts of Jesus' life. After all, there are twenty-seven books of the New Testament, and only four of these are Gospels. What about the other twenty-three?

Unfortunately, these other books yield very little information about Jesus' life, as they were written for other reasons and about different topics. There are *occasional* references to the things that Jesus said and did in the writings of Paul (thirteen letters go under his name in the New Testament), who informs us that Jesus was born of a woman (this datum is not of much use, of course, since it's hard to imagine the alternative), had twelve followers and several brothers (one of whom was named James), ministered to Jews, instituted the Lord's Supper, was handed over to the authorities, and was crucified.[6] And Paul does mention a couple of sayings of Jesus, one about paying preachers and the other about not getting divorced (1 Cor. 9:14; 7:11). But beyond that, Paul doesn't say much about Jesus' life and teachings. And the other New Testament authors say even less: they had other agendas they were pursuing and were not concerned to give the details of Jesus' life.

And so, whether we like it or not, whether we are Christian believers or not, whether we are historians or televangelists or preachers or Sunday school teachers or just regular lay folk with an interest in knowing about the life of Jesus (and about such things as his alleged marriage to Mary Magdalene), whatever our situation and whatever our personal beliefs, we are more or less restricted to the Gospels of the New Testament in trying to learn what Jesus said and did.

The Gospels of the New Testament

But even these accounts, as we have seen, are not problem-free for historians interested in knowing what really happened. To this extent, Leigh Teabing is absolutely right: these Gospels are not disinterested historical records that simply report what actually took place. The Gospels of the New Testament—even though they are our earliest and best accounts of Jesus' life—were written by later followers who wanted to put their own slant on the narratives that they relate.

Most people—readers of *The Da Vinci Code* and most others as well—probably don't realize this, but simply assume that Matthew, Mark, Luke, and John present historically accurate narratives of the things that Jesus said and did. But scholars have long recognized that this is not the case, that even these Gospels are problematic as historical sources (even if they are *not* seen as problematic as theological documents of the church, indicating what believers are to think about the importance of Jesus' life and the significance of his death).

But aren't these accounts written by eyewitnesses, people who were actually there to see Jesus say and do the things that are recounted in their narratives? As I've already indicated, that does not appear to be the case. In fact, contrary to what you might think, these Gospels don't even claim to be written by eyewitnesses.

We call these books, of course, Matthew, Mark, Luke, and John. And for centuries Christians have believed they were actually written by these people: two of the disciples of Jesus, Matthew the tax collector (see Matt. 9:9) and John, the "beloved disciple" (John 21:24), and two companions of the apostles, Mark, the secretary of Peter, and Luke, the traveling companion of Paul. These are, after all, the names found in the titles of these books. But what most people don't realize is that these titles were added later, by second-century Christians, decades after the books themselves had been written, in order to be able to claim that they were apostolic in origin. Why would later Christians do this? Recall our earlier discussion of the formation of the New Testament canon: only those books that were apostolic could be included. What was one to do with Gospels that were widely read and accepted as authoritative but that in fact were written anonymously, as all four of the New Testament Gospels were? They had to be associated with apostles in order to be included in the canon, and so apostolic names were attached to them.

But the books themselves were anonymous (no names attached). Read them for yourself with this in mind, and you'll see. Nowhere in these books are there any first-person narratives, where the authors say something like "Then Jesus and I went up to Jerusalem, and there we. . ." These books always talk in the third person, about what *other* people were doing—even the Gospels of Matthew and John, which allegedly were written by participants in Jesus' ministry.[7] And the titles are obviously not original parts of the books. Whoever called the first Gospel "the Gospel according to Matthew" was someone *other* than the author, someone who is telling us who, in his opinion, wrote the book. If the author was giving his book a title, he would not have

said who the book was "according to"; he would have called it
something like "the Gospel of Jesus Christ."

Moreover, as I pointed out, these four authors are all highly
trained, Greek-speaking Christians living near the end of the
first century, not the Aramaic-speaking peasants that Jesus had
as his own disciples.

This does not make the Gospels inaccurate, of course. They
could have been written later, by non-eyewitnesses, and still preserved the historical facts of Jesus' life. But there are solid reasons for thinking that in addition to giving some historical facts,
these books also alter the facts in order to make important religious claims about Jesus. For now, though, it is enough to note
that the books were written not by Jesus' own followers but by
later Christians.

Since even they had to have sources for their accounts of Jesus
(since everyone who says anything about him either needs to have
a source or has made it up), where did they get their information?
Fortunately, one of the authors, Luke (I'll continue to call them
by their traditional names, even though we don't know their real
identity), indicates at the beginning of his Gospel what he had
used as sources: earlier written accounts about Jesus and oral traditions that had been in circulation about him (Luke 1:1–4). It is
unfortunate that most of these earlier written sources have disappeared. But they have not disappeared without a trace. Scholars
are convinced that they know of two sources that were available
to Luke and his fellow evangelist Matthew.[8] The first, strikingly
enough, is the Gospel of Mark. Since the nineteenth century,
New Testament scholars have recognized that Mark was our
first Gospel written, possibly around 65 or 70 CE, and that both
Matthew and Luke, writing ten or fifteen years later, used Mark
for many of their stories about Jesus. That's why all three Gos-

pels tell so many of the same stories, often in exactly the same words. How could there be so much verbatim agreement among these three accounts of Jesus life? Two of them were copying the third for some of their stories.

But Matthew and Luke have other stories in common not found in Mark. Where did these come from? This is where the theory of a now-lost Gospel, Q, comes into play. This was not, as Leigh Teabing claims, a Gospel written by Jesus' own hand as a chronicle of his ministry. Q is the designation used by New Testament scholars to refer to a hypothetical source, available to both Matthew and Luke (though not to Mark and John), that contained many of the most memorable teachings of Jesus, including the Lord's Prayer and the Beatitudes, which are found in Matthew and Luke but not in Mark. (Q is an abbreviation for *Quelle*, the German word meaning "source.")

The reason that Matthew, Mark, and Luke are so much alike in their stories, then, is because they used some of the same sources. But Matthew and Luke each have unique stories not found in any other Gospel as well. Scholars have posited, then, that each of these authors had access to other sources no longer surviving, earlier written and oral accounts of the things Jesus said and did, usually designated M (Matthew's special source) and L (Luke's special source).

But what about John? John's Gospel is very different from the other three. Outside of the passion narrative (the account of Jesus' suffering and death), most of the sayings and deeds of Jesus found in John are found only in John, just as most of those in the earlier three Gospels are *not* found in John. John, then, must have had at his disposal other written and oral sources, which also no longer survive.[9]

P^{52}, a fragment of the Gospel of John (18:31–33, 37–38) discovered in a trash heap in the sands of Egypt. This credit-card-sized scrap is the earliest surviving manuscript of the New Testament, dating from around 125–150 CE. Both front and back are pictured here.

I have discussed the written sources lying behind our four Gospels. But where did these now lost written sources get *their* stories? Ultimately, since the followers of Jesus were not writing down the things he said and did during his life, the stories about Jesus must go back to oral traditions in circulation about him. In other words, after (or even before) Jesus' death, his disciples told stories about his life as they remembered it; then the people to whom they told these stories told the stories to others, and these others told stories to more people, who told stories to still others. This oral circulation of the accounts of Jesus' life went on for years—decades—until someone bothered to write down the stories (e.g., Mark and Q). Ultimately, then, our earliest surviving written accounts, and the written sources they were dependent on, go back to stories that were being passed around by word of mouth for year after year, decade after decade.

It is this that causes special problems for historians who want to know what actually happened in the life of Jesus. We don't have written records from his own day, only later accounts written by people who had heard the stories that had been in circulation for so many years. What happens, though, to stories as they circulate by word of mouth? Did you, or your kids, ever play the party game telephone? Kids all sit in a circle, one kid whispers a story to the one sitting next to her, who tells it to the one next to her, and so on, around the circle, until it comes back to the first kid—and by then it's a different story. (If it weren't a different story every time, it would be a pretty pointless game to play.)

Imagine playing telephone not just in a living room among a dozen kids who are all from the same time and place and who all speak the same language, but among hundreds of people living in different countries, speaking different languages, living in different contexts with different needs and different problems—all telling the stories in light of their own situations. What would happen to the stories? Some of them may remain relatively intact, but lots of them would change, and change drastically. Some other stories would be made up for the occasion and then be told and retold until they too were changed.

Could such a thing have happened to the stories of Jesus, in circulation throughout the Roman empire during the years and decades after his death, before they were written down? Not only are scholars of antiquity sure that such a thing could have happened, but they have evidence to indicate that in fact it did happen. The evidence resides in the stories as they came to be written down. As I've pointed out, some of the Gospels tell the stories of Jesus word for word the same way (since they used the same sources). But lots of stories are different in the various accounts we have. Some of the stories are just slightly different as one detail or another has come to be changed. But some of the stories are enormously different. And some of the stories were obviously made up. Everyone agrees on this—otherwise they'd have to say that Jesus really was in the habit of zapping his playmates as a five-year-old and that he really did emerge from his tomb tall as a skyscraper. But these things didn't happen. Where, then, did the stories come from? They had to have been made up.

Even the accounts of the New Testament Gospels contain stories that have been radically changed or even made up. This becomes abundantly clear once you read the stories found in the different Gospels and compare them in detail with one another. When Jesus was born, was his family originally from Nazareth (as in Luke) or from Bethlehem (as in Matthew)? Did Joseph and Mary flee to Egypt after his birth (as in Matthew) or return to Nazareth about a month later (as in Luke)? If there was a worldwide census for all people to be taxed (as in Luke), why does no other ancient source mention it (including Matthew)? And how can we imagine a census such as Luke describes, where everyone returns to their ancestral home to register for a tax, so that Joseph returns to Bethlehem, where his ancestor David was born a thousand years earlier? If we had a census like this today, and you had to return to the home of your ancestors a thousand years ago, where would *you* go? What about Jesus' death? Why does John indicate that Jesus died the day the Passover meal was being prepared (John 19:14) but Mark indicate that he died the day after it had been eaten (Mark 14:12; 15:25)? Why does Mark indicate that Simon of Cyrene carried Jesus' cross (Mark 15:21) but John indicate that Jesus carried it the entire way himself (John 19:27)? Why does Mark indicate that Jesus said nothing throughout the entire proceeding, as if he was in shock, but Luke indicate that he had numerous conversations both en route to crucifixion and while he was hanging on the cross? And what about Jesus' ministry? Why does Matthew indicate that Jesus refused to produce a sign to prove his identity (Matt. 12:38–39) when according to John, Jesus spent most of his public ministry doing just that (John 4:54; 20:31)? Why do the disciples never understand who Jesus is in Mark's Gospel but recognize it right away in John's? Why does Jesus never discuss his identity in Mark but spend all of his discourses discussing practically nothing else in John? Why does Jesus cleanse the Temple at the end of his life in the earlier three Gospels when it is virtually the first thing he does in his ministry in John?

We could go on nearly forever pointing out the differences among our Gospels, but instead I'll simply refer you to other discussions of the matter.[10] Here I want simply to emphasize that since our Gospels are rooted in oral traditions about Jesus' life, the accounts we have represent stories that were changed over time as they were told and retold, year after year, until Christian authors near the end of the first century wrote them down.

This includes stories about Jesus and his followers—not just his male followers, the twelve disciples, but also his female followers, including Mary Magdalene. Given the nature of our sources, how can we actually know how Jesus interacted with people? How can we know, for example, how he treated women? Or the extent to which he was involved with Mary Magdalene? Or whether he was ever married? Or whether he ever had sex and produced a child? Given the fact that the New Testament

Gospels are our most reliable sources, and yet they themselves are problematic from a historical point of view, how do we establish what Jesus actually did, said, and experienced in his life?

Obviously we need to have some fairly rigorous historical criteria in place if we expect to extract reliable information from sources such as these. In the next chapter, I'll explain what criteria scholars have devised in their attempts to establish the facts of Jesus' life, and then in the chapter that follows I'll show how these facts are of relevance in dealing with the claims of *The Da Vinci Code* that Jesus had close contact with his female followers, including Mary Magdalene, to whom he was supposedly married and with whom he supposedly produced an offspring.

Chapter Six

The Historical Jesus of Our Sources

Throughout *The Da Vinci Code* there are statements made about the historical Jesus—he is said to have been a mortal prophet, to have been married to Mary Magdalene, to have produced a child with her, to have given her the instructions about how to carry on his ministry in the church after his death, and so on.

As Teabing informs Sophie early on in their conversation in his drawing room:

> "My dear," Teabing declared, "until *that* moment in history, Jesus was viewed by His followers as a mortal prophet . . . a great and powerful man, but a *man* nonetheless. A mortal."
>
> "Not the Son of God?"
>
> "Right," Teabing said. "Jesus' establishment as 'the Son of God' was officially proposed and voted on by the Council of Nicaea." (p. 233)

Later he indicates that Jesus was not merely a mortal prophet but was fully human with serious, human relationships, including a most significant one with Mary Magdalene, despite the attempts of later church writers to cover it up:

"As I mentioned," Teabing clarified, "the early Church needed to convince the world that the mortal prophet Jesus was a *divine* being. Therefore, any gospels that described *earthly* aspects of Jesus' life had to be omitted from the Bible. Unfortunately for the early editors, one particularly troubling earthly theme kept recurring in the gospels. Mary Magdalene." He paused. "More specifically, her marriage to Jesus Christ." (p. 244)

The Harvard symbologist Robert Langdon also maintains that Jesus was probably married:

"Jesus as a married man makes infinitely more sense than our standard biblical view of Jesus as a bachelor."
"Why?" Sophie asked.
"Because Jesus was a Jew," Langdon said. . . . "According to Jewish custom, celibacy was condemned, and the obligation for a Jewish father was to find a suitable wife for his son. If Jesus were not married, at least one of the Bible's gospels would have mentioned it and offered some explanation for His unnatural state of bachelorhood." (p. 245)

According to Teabing and Langdon, not only was Jesus married to Mary Magdalene, but he planned for her, not Peter, to carry on his mission to establish the Christian church. As Teabing interprets a key passage in one of the noncanonical Gospels:

"At this point in the gospels, Jesus suspects He will soon be captured and crucified. So He gives Mary Magdalene instructions on how to carry on His church after He is gone. . . . According to these unaltered gospels, it was not *Peter* to whom Christ gave directions with which to establish the Christian Church. It was *Mary Magdalene*." (pp. 247–48)

Not only was Mary to continue Jesus' ministry in the church, but she was the one through whom the bloodline of Jesus would be kept alive. For she, in fact, carried his child:

"According to the Priory," Teabing continued, "Mary Magdalene was pregnant at the time of the crucifixion. For the safety of Christ's unborn child, she had no choice but to flee the Holy Land." (p. 255)

Is there any historical truth in any of these assertions about Jesus and Mary, or are they simply part of the literary fiction of *The Da Vinci Code*? The only way to get to the bottom of the problem is to ask a more basic question: how do we know anything about the historical Jesus?

As we saw in the last chapter, our only recourse for knowing something about Jesus, or about anyone else in the past, is to consider our sources of information. Our principal sources for Jesus, as we have seen, are the Gospels of the New Testament, and possibly a few of the noncanonical Gospel accounts that may also provide useful information about his life. But these sources cannot be used uncritically, for, as we have seen, even our earliest sources (for example, Mark and the hypothetical document Q) were written decades after the events they describe and were based on oral traditions that had been in circulation year after year among people who modified the stories they told and re-told about Jesus' life. This means that *all* of our sources need to be taken with a pound of salt. We need to approach them cautiously, carefully, and methodically if we are to extract historically reliable information about them, for what we are after is not the *changed* accounts of Jesus' life but the *original* information: what Jesus really said, did, and experienced in his life.

How can we learn such information, so as to evaluate the claims made by the likes of Leigh Teabing or Robert Langdon (or Dan Brown, or anyone else who says anything at all about the historical Jesus)? There are in fact scholars who have devoted their entire lives to dealing with this problem of how to know what really happened in the life of Jesus. These are highly trained scholars of the ancient world who read all the sources in their original languages (Greek, Aramaic, Latin, etc.), are familiar with every trace of a mention of Jesus in our ancient accounts, and have devised methods for sifting through all the material in order to determine what is historically reliable and what is not. The vast bulk of the scholarship produced by these experts is far from scintillating—it is hard-hitting, rigorous, detailed, highly nuanced stuff, of use to, and interest to, mostly other scholars in the field. But the conclusions that scholars have reached can in fact be fascinating to a nonexpert audience. What I will try to do here is to put the methods scholars have devised for reconstructing the life of Jesus in simple and accessible terms, with the understanding that there has been a serious amount of blood, sweat, and sheer hard work lying behind this rather simple presentation.

Our Methods for Reconstructing the Life of the Historical Jesus

Scholars by and large agree on several criteria to be used with our surviving sources to help figure out what really happened in Jesus' life. The following four criteria are among the most important.[1]

The Earlier the Better
Since the stories about Jesus—including those in which he has some involvement with Mary Magdalene and others—were changed as they were told and retold over time, in light of the beliefs, worldviews, and perspectives of the people telling the stories, then the earliest sources by and large will provide information that is less likely to have been radically changed than the later sources. The reason is obvious: for the earliest sources there will

have been less time to change the accounts than for the later sources. That's why scholars working to uncover what actually happened in Jesus' life tend to use Mark and Q, for example, more extensively than they use John and Thomas. These latter two were created decades after the former two, and so are less likely to retain historically reliable information.

Still, since all our sources are *relatively* late (i.e., they are not contemporaneous with Jesus himself), it simply will not do to accept what the earliest ones say as historically reliable. They too contain stories changed in the process of retelling. And so other criteria are also necessary.

Piling on the Testimonies

Scholars who try to reconstruct the events of Jesus' life are significantly helped when they find early sources that *independently* provide the same information about him. If two or more independent sources give the same account about something in Jesus' life, then neither one of these sources could have made it up, but the information, in this case, must have come from a yet earlier source—possibly from an actual historical datum of Jesus' life. It is important to stress, however, that for this criterion to work, the sources need to be independent of one another. If there is a story that is found in Matthew, Mark, and Luke, for example, that would *not* be a datum independently attested in three sources, since Matthew and Luke would have gotten the story from Mark. In that case we have only *one* source for the story, not several. But if there is a story, say, found in Mark, Q, and Thomas, all of which *are* independent of one another, the story must have been from a yet earlier source, available to them all.

Let me give a couple of examples. (1) Jesus is said to have had brothers in independent sources: Paul, Mark, John, and even

Josephus. Conclusion? Jesus probably had brothers. (2) Jesus is connected with John the Baptist in Mark, Q, and John. It appears, then, that Jesus really did have a connection with John. (3) Jesus is said to have publicly associated with women in Mark, L (Luke's special source), John, and Thomas. Conclusion?

Cutting Against the Grain

Since the stories about Jesus were obviously changed in light of the perspectives, worldviews, and interests of the people telling the stories, what do we do with information about him found in our sources that cuts *against the grain* of these perspectives, worldviews, and interests? Traditions of this kind, which seem contrary to what Christians would have wanted to say about Jesus, are obviously not traditions that they would have made up. And so traditions of that sort are especially valuable, since they are not invented traditions but appear to represent things that really happened in Jesus' life.

For example, it is independently attested that Jesus came from Nazareth (Mark, John). And this cuts against what Christians would have wanted to say about him, since the messiah was supposed to come from *Bethlehem* (which is why we have stories about him being born there). But why would Christians say he came from Nazareth? Prior to Christianity, Nazareth was a one-horse town that almost no one had even *heard* of. The Christians who told the stories of Jesus got no mileage out of claiming he came from such a tiny, unknown, and inauspicious hamlet in the backwoods of Galilee. And so the stories that place him there are probably authentic—that is where he was from. Or consider Jesus' baptism by John: early Christians understood that in the rite of baptism, the person baptizing was spiritually superior to the one being baptized. Why, then, would a Christian make up the idea that Jesus was baptized by someone else? Wouldn't that be open to the understanding that John was superior to Jesus? Since Christians who revered Jesus would not invent such a tale, it is probably something that actually happened.

Context Is (Almost) Everything

Finally, scholars take very seriously the conclusion reached nowadays by *everyone* who studies the historical Jesus: that he was a Jew living in first-century Palestine. If there are stories about what Jesus said and did that cannot be plausibly fit into that context, then it is nigh impossible to think that those stories are historically accurate. (Langford himself, after all, invokes something like this historical criterion when he indicates that Jesus would probably not have been a Jewish bachelor.) Sayings of Jesus, for example, that make better sense in some *other* context probably derive from that other context, rather than from Jesus' own life.

For example, a number of the sayings of Jesus found in the Coptic Gospel of Thomas or in other writings of the Nag Hammadi Library have a definite Gnostic slant. The problem is that we have no evidence to suggest that Gnosticism could be found already in the first two decades of the first century—especially in rural Galilee. These Gnostic sayings must be later traditions, then, placed on Jesus' lips in some other context (e.g., in the second century, in a place such as Egypt or Syria). That is not to hold that all of Thomas's sayings need to be ruled out of court. Even in this Gospel, for example, Jesus tells the parable of the mustard seed, a parable also told (independently) by Mark. There is nothing particularly Gnostic about the saying, and it is found in two independent sources, one of which is very early. Conclusion? Jesus may well have spoken it.

These, then, are some of the main criteria that scholars use to examine the earliest sources that we have for the life of Jesus. Knowing what he said and did is not simply a matter of "taking someone's word for it" or of accepting everything (or anything) said about him in our Gospel sources. Every word of Jesus, everything he allegedly did, and everything he is said to have experienced (including, for example, a claim that he was married) has to be subjected to these criteria in order to see whether it plausibly can be attributed to the historical circumstances of his life or not. Sayings and deeds of Jesus that do not meet these criteria simply cannot be accepted as historical. In short, knowing about Jesus is not a matter of sheer guesswork, creative imagination, or wishful thinking. It is a matter of looking at our sources with a critical eye to determine what really happened in his life.

In the next chapter we will be considering the claims made in *The Da Vinci Code* about Jesus being married, having a sexual relationship with Mary Magdalene, and intending for her to establish his church. Before going there, however, it is important to summarize what can be known about Jesus' life in broader terms, since the character of his life in general will play an important role in our understanding of many of the specifics.

Jesus as an Apocalyptic Prophet

On more than one occasion, Leigh Teabing insists that prior to Constantine, Jesus was recognized as a "mortal prophet," except in our New Testament Gospels, which portray him as divine. As we have seen, Teabing is wrong on a couple of points. He is wrong to think that the New Testament portrays Jesus only as divine, as Jesus is portrayed here too, in many passages, as mortal. And he is wrong to think that the earlier understanding of Jesus changed with Constantine: Constantine had almost nothing to do with the developing sense that in addition to being human, Jesus was also divine. This happened centuries before Constantine's day. But Teabing is right on one key issue: our earliest and best sources do indeed understand Jesus to be a mortal prophet. In fact, more than that, they understand him to be a prophet who made a precise set of prophecies. Jesus, like the Essenes of the Dead Sea Scrolls community that we examined in chapter 2, was an apocalyptic Jew, who understood that God was soon to intervene in the course of history to overthrow the forces of evil in this world and to establish a new kingdom on earth, in which there would be no more pain and suffering. This view of Jesus as an apocalypticist derives from a careful examination of our earliest surviving sources, as I will show. And it is key to evaluating some of the claims of *The Da Vinci Code*—for example, that Jesus was married and sexually active.

In chapter 2 we saw some of the features of the Jewish apocalyptic worldview. Jews who held this view maintained that there were two fundamental components of reality, the forces of good and the forces of evil, with God and his angels on one side and the Devil and his demons on the other. This dualism was worked out in a historical scheme in which this current evil age would be succeeded by a good age to come, in which God would bring in his own kingdom and rule supreme. The coming of this kingdom would involve a cataclysmic event in which God would destroy the forces of evil in an act of judgment, and people too would be judged, depending on whether they sided with God or the forces of evil in this wicked age. Moreover, these Jews believed all this would happen very soon.

Since the early part of the twentieth century many scholars have recognized that this was the view of the historical Jesus himself. Evidence comes from our early sources of Jesus' life—the surviving Christian Gospels—as these are examined in light of the criteria I have laid out above.[2] Traditions of Jesus as an apocalypticist are found in our earliest accounts, such as Mark and Q and M and L (though not in our later accounts, including John and Thomas), which were all independent of one another. In these traditions Jesus anticipates that God would soon send a judge from heaven, whom he calls by the enigmatic designation "the Son of Man," who will wreak havoc among the forces of evil, destroying all that stands opposed to God and bringing in God's good kingdom for those who have sided with God in this wicked age. Consider what Jesus says in our earliest (independently attested) sources, for example:

> Whoever is ashamed of me and of my words in this adulterous and sinful generation, of that one will the Son of Man be ashamed when he comes in the glory of his Father with the holy angels. . . . Truly I tell you, there are some standing here who will not taste death until they see that the kingdom of God has come in power. (Mark 8:38–9:1)
>
> And in those days, after that affliction, the sun will grow dark and the moon will not give its light, and the stars will be falling from heaven, and the powers in the sky will be shaken; and then they will see the Son of Man coming on the clouds with great power and glory. And then he will send forth his angels and he will gather his elect from the four winds, from the end of earth to the end of heaven. . . . Truly I tell you, this generation will not pass away before all these things take place. (Mark 13:24–27, 30)
>
> For just as the flashing lightning lights up the earth from one part of the sky to the other, so will the Son of Man be in his day. . . . And just as it was in the days of Noah, so will it be in the days of the Son of Man. They were eating, drinking, marrying, and giving away in marriage, until the day that Noah went into the

ark and the flood came and destroyed them all. So too will it be on the day when the Son of Man is revealed. (Q, via Luke 17:24; 26–27, 30; cf. Matt. 24:27, 37–39)

And you, be prepared, because you do not know the hour when the Son of Man is coming. (Q, via Luke 12:39; Matt. 24:44)

Just as the weeds are gathered and burned with fire, so will it be at the culmination of the age. The Son of Man will send forth his angels, and they will gather from his kingdom every cause of sin and all who do evil, and they will cast them into the furnace of fire. In that place there will be weeping and gnashing of teeth. Then the righteous will shine forth as the sun, in the kingdom of their father. (M, via Matt. 13:40–43)

But take care for yourselves so that your hearts are not over-come with wild living and drunkenness and the cares of this life, and that day come upon you unexpectedly, like a sprung trap. For it will come to all those sitting on the face of the earth. Be alert at all times, praying to have strength to flee from all these things that are about to take place and to stand in the presence of the Son of Man. (L, via Luke 21:34–36)

There are lots of sayings of this sort in our traditions: I have picked just a few examples here. I should stress that these apocalyptic sayings of Jesus are from our earliest sources (recall that the earlier the better), they are independently attested, and they are completely credible contextually (recall that similar views were found in the Dead Sea Scrolls in Jesus' own day). More-over, some apocalyptic sayings of Jesus cut against the grain of what early Christians would have said if they were putting words on Jesus' lips. Consider the following saying from Q:

Truly I say to you, in the renewed world, when the Son of Man is sitting on the throne of his glory, you [disciples] also will be seated on twelve thrones, judging the twelve tribes of Israel. (Matt. 19:28; cf. Luke 22:30)

Why would a later Christian not have made up this saying? Notice that Jesus is speaking to all twelve of his disciples and indicates that they will *all* be rulers in the future kingdom that is coming. But that would have been obviously a difficult claim for *later* Christians to make about the twelve disciples, after the events of Jesus' death had taken place, for Christians knew that one of Jesus' disciples, Judas Iscariot, had betrayed Jesus. Is Judas going to be one of the rulers of the future kingdom? Christians obviously would not have thought so. Then why did they preserve a saying of Jesus that indicated he would be? Evidently this is something that Jesus really did say, and they preserved his saying intact without changing it in light of their own perspective.

Specific Apocalyptic Teachings of Jesus

Later we will see how the apocalyptic message of Jesus relates to the claims made about him in *The Da Vinci Code*. For now it is important to see in a little more detail what scholars have determined about his proclamation. It is important to recall that I am not here simply summarizing what the Gospels say about Jesus. The later Gospel writers had a somewhat different view of him, as they were basing their understanding on the traditions about Jesus that had been in circulation by word of mouth for decades before they had received these traditions and written them down. I am interested here in what the *historical* Jesus himself actually said and did, as based on a critical evaluation of our earliest sources, using the criteria I have spelled out above. The traditions found in later sources—for example, the claims in the Gospel of John that Jesus called himself divine—are not found in our earliest sources and do not at all cut against the grain of what the earliest Christians would have wanted to say about him. They are therefore not reliable as historical data. But other materials found in our traditions are reliable, and it is these that I want to summarize.

It is clear that the historical Jesus talked about the coming kingdom of God. As his teaching is summarized in our earliest surviving Gospel account, that of Mark:

> The time is filled up and the kingdom of God is almost here; repent and believe in the good news! (Mark 1:15)

When Jesus talks about the coming kingdom of God in this verse, and in other sayings that can safely be attributed to him, it appears that he is talking not about a spiritual kingdom (or about going to heaven when you die) but about an actual physical presence of God here on earth. As he says in a saying preserved in Q:

> And there will be weeping and gnashing of teeth when you see Abraham and Isaac and Jacob and all the prophets in the kingdom, but you are cast out; and people will come from east and west and from north and south and recline at table in the kingdom of God. (Q, via Luke 13:23–29; cf. Matt. 8:11–12)

Such references to a real, physical kingdom of God are found throughout our earliest records of Jesus. Like other apocalypticists living before him and afterward, Jesus evidently thought that God was going to extend his rule from the heavenly realm where he resides down here to earth. There would be a real, physical kingdom here, a paradisal world in which God himself would rule his faithful people, where there would be eating, drinking, and talking, where there would be human rulers sitting on thrones (the twelve disciples) and human members of the kingdom eating at banquets.

This coming kingdom would involve a massive judgment on the earth, as Jesus indicated in a number of his parables—including this one, found in slightly different forms in both Matthew and Thomas:

Again, the kingdom of heaven is like a net which was thrown
into the sea and gathered fish of every kind. When it was full,
they hauled it ashore, and sitting down chose the good fish and
put them into containers, but the bad fish they threw away. That's
how it will be at the completion of the age. The angels will come
and separate the evil from the midst of the righteous, and cast
them into the fiery furnace. There people will weep and gnash
their teeth. (Matt. 13:47–50)

Or as is found in M, Matthew's special source:

Just as the weeds are gathered and burned with fire, so will it
be at the culmination of the age. The Son of Man will send forth
his angels, and they will gather from his kingdom every cause of
sin and all who do evil, and they will cast them into the furnace
of fire. In that place there will be weeping and gnashing of teeth.
Then the righteous will shine forth as the sun, in the kingdom of
their father. (Matt. 13:40–43)

This coming judgment, as we have seen, would be a cosmic
event, brought about by the figure that Jesus calls the Son of Man:

And in those days, after that affliction, the sun will grow dark
and the moon will not give its light, and the stars will be falling
from heaven, and the powers in the sky will be shaken; and they
will see the Son of Man coming on the clouds with great power
and glory. And then he will send forth his angels and he will
gather his elect from the four winds, from the end of earth to the
end of heaven. (Mark 13:24–27)

But who are these elect who will survive the coming onslaught
and enter into his kingdom? Since the age we live in now is evil,
with evil powers in control, the people who are now high and
mighty are those who will be judged when the Son of Man arrives. It is the lowly, the downtrodden, the oppressed who will
inherit the good kingdom that is coming. For God is on the side
of those who stand up for him, who are, as a result, oppressed by

the evil powers in control of this world. As Jesus is recorded as saying:

> And people will come from east and west and from north and south and recline in the kingdom of God; and behold, those who are last will be first and the first will be last. (Luke 13:29–30; this may be Q—see Matt. 20:16)

That is why Jesus took the side of the outcasts in his public ministry. They were the ones who would inherit God's kingdom when it arrived. This kingdom would come not for the rich and powerful but for the poor and lowly. And that is why Jesus urged his followers not to strive for wealth or prominence but to devote themselves to lives of service for others, for it was those who were lowly now who would be exalted in the coming kingdom. Thus, from our earliest surviving source, Jesus is recorded as saying:

> If anyone wishes to be first, he will be last of all and the servant of all. (Mark 9:35)

And also:

> You know that those who are thought to rule over the nations exercise full power over them and their mighty rulers utilize their great authority over them. But it will not be so among you. But whoever wishes to be great among you will be your servant, and the one who wishes to be first among you will be the slave of all. (Mark 10:42–44)

These sayings will be relevant when we consider the view that Jesus had of women, in the next chapter. For women in Jesus' day were among those considered lowly, who from our standards today were oppressed as second-rate persons, under the authority of the men (their fathers or husbands) who were to

This is one of the
earliest paintings of
Jesus to survive from
antiquity (from about
two centuries after
Jesus' death), from the
catacomb of San
Callisto in Rome.

have power in his world. But for Jesus, the powerless would be
the ones who inherited the kingdom.

This theme of reversal gets played out in some of Jesus' most
familiar teachings, the so-called Beatitudes, which tend, unfortunately, to be ripped out of their original apocalyptic contexts
by people who quote them. The Beatitudes are a group of sayings attributed to Jesus in a variety of our sources in which he
pronounces blessings on certain groups of people (the term *be-
atitude* itself comes from the Latin beatus, "blessed"). The best-
known of these sayings are found in Matthew's Sermon on the
Mount, which begins:

> Blessed are the poor in spirit, for theirs is the kingdom of heaven;
> blessed are those who mourn, for they will be comforted; blessed
> are those who are meek, for they will inherit the earth; blessed are
> those who hunger and thirst for righteousness, for they will be sat-
> isfied. (Matt. 5:3–6)

What many readers have not noticed in these sayings is the verb tenses. They describe what certain groups of people are experiencing in the present and what they *will* experience in the future. *Will* experience? When? Not in some vague, remote, and uncertain moment—sometime in the sky by and by. It will happen when the kingdom arrives. Those who are lowly, poor, and oppressed now will have their reward then.

A number of these sayings in Matthew are actually derived from Q. Interestingly, in Luke's version they tend to emphasize physical hardship more than internal struggles. For instance, rather than blessing the "poor in spirit," in Luke Jesus blesses "you who are poor" (i.e., those who are literally impoverished). Rather than speaking of those who "hunger and thirst for righteousness," in Luke Jesus speaks of those who "hunger and thirst." There are good reasons for thinking that in these instances Luke's version is closer to what Jesus himself may have said. For one thing, we find a very similar form of the sayings independently attested in the Gospel of Thomas:

> Blessed are the poor, for yours is the kingdom of heaven. (Gosp. Thom. 54)
> Blessed are those who are hungry, for the belly of the one who desires will be filled. (Gosp. Thom. 69)
> Blessed are you when you are hated and persecuted; no place will be found where you are persecuted. (Gosp. Thom. 68)

Interestingly, in Luke's version of the Beatitudes, these various apocalyptic blessings are followed by their counterparts, a set of apocalyptic woes:

> But woe to you who are wealthy, for you have your comfort [now]; woe to you who are full now, for you will go hungry. Woe to you who are rejoicing now, for you will mourn and weep. And

woe when everyone speaks well of you; for so too did your ancestors treat the false prophets. (Luke 6:24–26)

These particular apocalyptic judgments are not independently
attested in our other sources, but they certainly coincide with the
major themes we've already seen in this chapter. Jesus taught that
a day of judgment was coming with the appearance of the Son of
Man, who would bring a radical reversal: those who were presently
well-off would be condemned, and those who were suffering
would be blessed. Included in this apocalyptic message was a
warning of imminent destruction for all who did not heed Jesus'
words and turn to God as he wished.

But when would this take place? When would the Son of Man
arrive? When would the kingdom come? Would it be far off in the
distant future, years, decades, centuries, or millennia later? On the
contrary, as with most other Jewish apocalypticists of his day, Jesus
appears to have understood that the coming of God's kingdom was
imminent. As he says in our earliest surviving Gospel:

> Whoever is ashamed of me and of my words in this adulterous
> and sinful generation, of that one will the Son of Man be ashamed
> when he comes in the glory of his Father with the holy angels.
> Truly I tell you, *some of those who are standing here* will not taste
> death before they see that the kingdom of God has come in power.
> (Mark 8:38–9:1; emphasis added)
>
> Truly I tell you, *this generation* will not pass away until all these
> things have taken place. (Mark 13:30; emphasis added)
>
> Be awake, keep alert. For you don't know when that time is. It
> is like a man on a journey, who leaves his house and gives his
> slaves authority over their own work, and orders the doorkeeper
> to watch. Watch therefore—for you don't know when the mas-
> ter of the house is coming, whether in the evening, at midnight,
> at the crack of dawn, or in the morning—lest when he comes
> suddenly he finds you sleeping. But what I say to you I say to
> everyone: Watch! (Mark 13:33–37)

Or as he is recorded as saying in Q:

> But you should realize that if the homeowner knew the hour when the thief was coming, he would not allow him to dig a hole through the wall of his house; and you also, be prepared, for the Son of Man is coming in an hour that you are not expecting. (Luke 12:39–40; Matt. 24:43–44)

The imminence of the end of this age will be significant in the next chapter as well, as we will see how it appears to have affected Jesus' understanding of social relations in the present—including his understanding of the family and marriage—and consider Jesus' own life and the question of whether he was probably married and involved with a sexual relationship.

In sum, it appears, based on a critical review of our earliest surviving sources, that like the members of the Dead Sea Scrolls community before him (and like John the Baptist, whom we have not discussed here, but who was also an earlier apocalypticist), and like many of his first-generation followers after him (e.g., the apostle Paul), Jesus was an apocalyptic prophet who anticipated that God would soon intervene in the course of history in an act of judgment that would destroy all the evil that stands over against him and bring in his good, utopian kingdom here on earth.

Conclusion

I have spent some time in this chapter explaining how historians go about establishing which materials in the Gospel sources available to us can be accepted as historically reliable, as opposed to the great bulk of these materials that represent modifications of the tradition by Christians who told and retold the stories of Jesus before they came to be written down, starting in the second half of the first century, by some of his second-generation followers. It is important to see how historians go about this kind of work, in order to make my overarching point: that knowing about Jesus is not simply guesswork, on one hand, or a matter of coming up with an imaginative idea, on the other hand. It is always easy for someone—anyone!—to come up with a speculative or sensationalist claim about Jesus: Jesus was married! Jesus had babies! Jesus was a magician! Jesus was a Marxist! Jesus was an armed revolutionary! Jesus was gay![3] And I am not denying that people are perfectly within their rights to make any claim they want about Jesus, whether sensationalist or cautious. But if historians are to accept such claims, they need to look at the *evidence*. The only reliable evidence we have comes from our earliest sources, and we can neither simply take these at face value nor just read between the lines in order to make the sources say what we want them to say. They have to be used critically, following established criteria and historical principles.

When that is done, we arrive at an understanding of Jesus that is historically plausible, that fits Jesus—his words, deeds, and experiences—within his own time frame without trying to make out that he fits perfectly well into our own. In many ways the picture of Jesus that emerges may seem strange to modern ears. For Jesus appears to have been a Jewish apocalypticist anticipating the end of this present evil age within his own generation. This may not be the Jesus we have learned about in Sunday school or seen in the stained-glass window, and it may not be the Jesus touted in popular fiction based on sensationalist claims. But it does appear to be the Jesus of history.

In the next chapter I will take the next step to see how this historically reconstructed view of Jesus relates to the claims of Leigh Teabing and Robert Langdon in *The Da Vinci Code* that Jesus not only had women followers but also had a wife and lover, Mary Magdalene, who bore him a child after his crucifixion.

Chapter Seven

Jesus, Mary Magdalene, and Marriage

One of the key historical figures in *The Da Vinci Code* is an early follower of Jesus, Mary Magdalene. As we learn in the course of the narrative, Mary was not simply one of Jesus' followers—she was his wife and lover, with whom he produced an offspring, a child who would begin a family line that continues down till today, protected by the members of a secret society, the Priory of Sion. I should point out that this understanding of Mary Magdalene and Jesus is not an original contribution of the fiction of Dan Brown. For much of his "information" Brown was dependent on an earlier best-seller of the 1980s, a book called *Holy Blood, Holy Grail*, which Brown explicitly mentions in his novel but which he does not acknowledge as the primary source for much of what he has to say about Mary Magdalene (and the Priory of Sion).[1] Nonetheless, anyone familiar with both books will see the high degree of dependence. *Holy Blood, Holy Grail* was written not by scholars of antiquity or the Middle Ages, but by independent researchers Michael Baigent, Richard Leigh, and Henry Lincoln, who came up with the sensationalist but historically discredited views about

Mary, Jesus, the Grail, and the Priory of Sion.[2] Since my primary concern is with *The Da Vinci Code* and the views it represents, I will not deal directly with *Holy Blood, Holy Grail*, other than to say that Dan Brown has simply taken over many of its claims wholesale in his fictional account of the search for the Grail by Robert Langdon and Sophie Neveu.

Many of these claims have to do with Mary Magdalene and "her marriage to Jesus Christ" (p. 244). As evidence of this marriage, the British aristocrat and Grail-seeker Leigh Teabing appeals to a Gospel that did not come to be included in the New Testament, the Nag Hammadi tractate known as the Gospel of Philip, in which it is said, "The companion of the Saviour is Mary Magdalene." Teabing then declares, "As any Aramaic scholar will tell you, the word *companion* in those days, literally meant *spouse*" (p. 246).

Teabing goes on to quote another noncanonical Gnostic Gospel, the Gospel of Mary, where the apostles Peter and Levi have a dispute over whether Jesus would have revealed the truth to Mary. Teabing explains:

> "At this point in the gospels, Jesus suspects He will soon be captured and crucified. So He gives Mary Magdalene instructions on how to carry on His church after He is gone. . . . According to these unaltered gospels, it was not *Peter* to whom Christ gave directions with which to establish the Christian Church. It was *Mary Magdalene*." (pp. 247–48)

In order to stress the importance of Mary for the history of the Christian church, Teabing shows Sophie Neveu a genealogy of the Jewish "Tribe of Benjamin"; she notices that Mary Magdalene is in the genealogy, and expresses her surprise: "She was of the House of Benjamin?" "Indeed," Teabing said. "Mary Magdalene was of royal descent" (p. 248). This would mean, he points out, that any child born to Christ and Mary Magdalene would have a very pure bloodline of royalty. And that's why leaders of the church tried to cover over the relationship she had with Jesus:

> "The threat Mary Magdalene posed to the men of the early church was potentially ruinous. Not only was she the woman to whom Jesus had assigned the task of founding the Church, but she also had physical proof that the Church's newly proclaimed *deity* had spawned a mortal bloodline. The Church, in order to defend itself against the Magdalene's power, perpetuated her image as a whore and buried evidence of Christ's marriage to her, thereby defusing any potential claims that Christ had a surviving bloodline and was a mortal prophet." (p. 254)

But the cover-up was not completely successful, according to the traditions preserved through the centuries by the mysterious Priory of Sion:

> "According to the Priory," Teabing continued, "Mary Magdalene was pregnant at the time of the crucifixion. For the safety of Christ's unborn child, she had no choice but to flee the Holy Land. With the help of Jesus' trusted uncle, Joseph of Arimathea, Mary Magdalene secretly traveled to France, then known as Gaul. There she found safe refuge in the Jewish community. It was here in France that she gave birth to a daughter. Her name was Sarah." (p. 255)

As with other statements made in *The Da Vinci Code*, there is more fictional license in these various claims than historical truth. Some of the statements are simply in error. To take just one obvious example: it is wrong to say that when the Gospel of Philip calls Mary Jesus' "companion" that the Aramaic word means "spouse." For one thing, the word that is used is not Aramaic. The Gospel of Philip is in Coptic. And even though the word used there for "companion" actually is a loan word from another language, the language, again, is not Aramaic but Greek. In other words, Aramaic has nothing to do with the saying. And to cap it all off, the Greek word that is used (*koinōnos*) in fact means not "spouse" (or "lover") but "companion" (it is commonly used of friends and associates).

Other claims that Teabing makes are equally erroneous, or at least without any historical foundation. But this leads to a consideration of the broader issues that are raised. When looking at the historical record, what can we say about Jesus' relationship with women? Was he married? Was his wife Mary Magdalene? If so, did he have a normal sexual relationship with her? Did they have a child together?

In order to answer these questions we have to shift from the realm of literary fiction to that of historical fact, and that means shifting from sensationalist claims to historical methodology. As we saw in the previous chapter, it is difficult to reconstruct what happened in Jesus' life. Historians interested in doing so know that it is not a matter simply of quoting a verse here or there that randomly occurs in some Gospel or the other, and then taking that verse as historically accurate. Doing history is far more complicated than that. We have to take into account the nature of our sources and to apply rigorous criteria to them in order to separate the facts from the fictions. That is to say, even if our early sources *did* claim that Jesus and Mary were lovers and/or married, we would have to examine these sources to see whether the claims were true. But as it turns out, Teabing's assertions notwithstanding, not a single one of our ancient sources indicates that Jesus was married, let alone married to Mary Magdalene. All such claims are part of modern fictional reconstructions of Jesus' life, not rooted in the surviving accounts themselves. The historical approach to our sources may not be as exciting and sensationalist as fictional claims about Jesus (he kept a lover! he had sex! he made babies!), but there's something to be said for knowing what really happened in history, even if it is not as titillating as what happens in novels.

And so there are a range of questions that I'd like to ask about the historical Jesus, moving from the broader to the narrower: What was his relationship generally with women? What role did they play in his ministry? Did he have a close relationship with any of them? Was he possibly married? And what exactly was his relationship with Mary Magdalene? Are there any historical indications that they were married? That they had sexual relations?

Men in the Ministry of Jesus

The first thing to be said is that it appears that most of Jesus' followers, and certainly his closest followers, were men. The vast majority of the stories about Jesus—both those that can be established as historically authentic and those about which we might have some doubts—concern his interaction with men. This is not to be unexpected: women in the first century were typically under the authority of the men in their lives—their fathers and/or husbands—and would not have been allowed, for the most part, to be traipsing about the countryside after an itinerant teacher when there was so much work to be done in the home: preparing food, making and mending clothes, taking care of children.[3] These were women's activities; men had more of a public profile outside the home. For a woman to be active outside the home usually meant either that she was not under a man's authority (father or husband) because she was, say, an older single adult or that she was an upper-class woman of means who had others, such as slaves, to take care of her household duties. And even though a select few of Jesus' followers may well have been from the upper classes—and probably were, as we will see—the vast majority of them were peasants. And peasant women in areas such as rural Galilee would necessarily have spent most of their time at home working; there was not a lot of time (if any) for leisure activities such as going out midweek to hear a good sermon.

And so it is no surprise that most of Jesus' followers were men, who were more likely to be out and about rather than stuck at home. Moreover, it is a firmly rooted tradition in our historical record that the *closest* followers of Jesus were all men. These are the twelve disciples, whose gender is not open to serious dispute—twelve men drawn from the larger company, predominantly of men, around Jesus. This was not only the actual situation attending Jesus' public ministry but also the ideal situation that he himself appears to have envisaged. For, as we have seen, one of the firmly grounded traditions of Jesus' teaching is that he expected the imminent arrival of the kingdom of God in which God would rule his people through human mediators. And who would those human mediators be? Recall the saying of Jesus preserved for us from Q, a saying that passes our historical criteria for authenticity: "Truly I say to you, in the renewed world, when the Son of Man is sitting on the throne of his glory, you [disciples] also will be seated on twelve thrones, judging the twelve tribes of Israel" (Matt. 19:28; cf. Luke 22:30). The future rulers of God's people would all be men.

Women in the Ministry of Jesus

This does not mean that women were absent from Jesus' ministry. Quite the contrary, even though women are not prominently featured in the stories of Jesus in comparison with men, they do appear there on a regular basis, far more than one might anticipate given the patriarchal society that restricted women's public activities in the first century. More than other teachers, including other Jewish teachers, Jesus appears to have been publicly involved with women in his ministry. This is born out by a careful examination of our surviving sources, utilizing the various historical criteria that I spelled out in the previous chapter.

To provide a brief synopsis of the material, I can summarize as follows.[4] It is attested independently in two of our early sources, Mark and L (Luke's special source) that Jesus was accompanied by women in his travels (Mark 15:40–41; Luke 8:1–3). This tradition is corroborated, independently again, by the Gospel of Thomas (e.g., Gosp. Thom. 114) and by other passages where Jesus interacts with women (e.g., Luke 10:38–42; Matt. 15:21–29). Mark and L also indicate that women provided Jesus with financial support during his ministry, evidently serving as his patrons (Mark 15:40–41; Luke 8:1–3). That is to say, since Jesus during his ministry had no source of income, these women (one of them is named as Mary Magdalene) provided him with the funds that he and his disciples needed in order to live. These obviously would have been wealthier women who would not have been forced to remain at home to do the work necessary to keep a household together. It may be that some of these women, including Mary Magdalene, were single, but not all of them were. One of them is named as "Joanna, the wife of [King] Herod's steward Chuza" (Luke 8:2). Another is called Susanna, but, as with Mary, we are not sure of her marital status. Luke tells us that there were "many others who provided for him [Jesus] out of their own resources." The others named by Mark include one named Salome and another Mary, who is identified as "the mother of James the younger and of Joses." It is possible that this is none other than the mother of Jesus, who is earlier said in Mark 6:3 to have two other sons named James and Joses. In any event, it is clear that Jesus was accompanied in his travels not only by the twelve men disciples but also by women, some of whom provided for him out of their means.

Not only was Jesus accompanied by women, he also was actively in contact with them during his public ministry. In both Mark and John, Jesus is said to have engaged in public dialogue and debate with women who were not among his immediate followers (John 4:1–42; Mark 7:24–30). Both Gospels also record, independently of one another, the tradition that Jesus had physical contact with a woman who anointed him with oil in public (Mark 14:3–9; John 12:1–8). In Mark's account this is an unnamed woman in the house of a leper named Simon (this same account is found in a different form in Luke as well, who appears to have gotten it from Mark but changed it in some key ways; see Luke 7:36–50); in John's account it is Mary of Bethany, the sister of Martha and Lazarus, in her own home. And Jesus is said to have helped women in need on several occasions (e.g., Matt. 15:21–29).

In all four of the canonical Gospels, the women who accompanied Jesus from Galilee to Jerusalem during the last week of his life are said to have been present at his crucifixion (Matt. 27:55; Mark 15:40–41; Luke 23:49; John 19:25). The earliest traditions in Mark suggest that they alone remained faithful to the end: all of his male disciples had fled. In addition, it is clear from all four of the canonical Gospels, along with the noncanonical Gospel of Peter, that women followers were the first to believe that Jesus' body was no longer in the tomb (Matt. 28:1–10; Mark 16:1–8; Luke 23:55–24:10; John 20:1–2; Gosp. Pet. 50–57). These accounts all differ in significant ways concerning how many women there were at the empty tomb: was it Mary Magdalene alone, as in John? Or Mary Magdalene and other women, as in the other Gospels? And if it was with other women, which other women? It depends on which account you read. In any event, it was these women who were the first to proclaim that Jesus had been raised from the dead. As some feminist historians have pointed out, it is hard to underestimate the importance of this tradition about the women at the tomb: without these women, there may well have been no proclamation of the resurrection—and thus no Christianity.

There are other interesting traditions about Jesus' contact with women that are found in only one or the other of our Gospels and so do not meet our criterion that multiply attested stories are more likely to be authentic. These would include the memorable moment found only in Luke's Gospel when Jesus encourages his friend Mary of Bethany in her decision to attend to his teaching rather than busy herself with "womanly" household duties (Luke 10:38–42).

What can we say about the contextual credibility of these traditions, in light of our criterion that any tradition about Jesus must plausibly be situated in a first-century Palestinian context to be accepted as historical? It is true that women were generally viewed as inferior to men in the ancient world. But there were exceptions: Greek philosophical schools such as the Epicureans and the Cynics, for example, advocated equality for women. Of course, there were not many Epicureans or Cynics in Jesus' immediate environment of Palestine, and our limited sources may suggest that women, as a rule, were generally even more restricted in that rural part of the empire with respect to their abilities to engage in social activities outside the home and away from the authority of their fathers or husbands. Is it credible, then, that a Jewish teacher would have encouraged and promoted such activities?

We have no solid evidence to suggest that other Jewish teachers had women followers during Jesus' day. But we do know that the Pharisees were supported and protected by powerful women in the court of King Herod the Great. Unfortunately, the few sources that we have say little about women among the lower classes, who did not have the wealth or standing to make them independent of their fathers or husbands.

There is one other consideration, however, that makes it easy to believe that Jesus may have had women publicly following him during his ministry. This involves the particular character of his proclamation of the coming kingdom of God. If you'll recall, Jesus maintained that God was going to intervene in history and bring about a reversal of fortunes. The first would be last, and the last would be first. Those who were rich would be impoverished, and the poor would be rich. Those who were exalted now would be humbled, and the humble would be exalted. As a corollary of his message, Jesus associated with the outcasts and downtrodden of society, evidently as an enactment of his proclamation that the kingdom would belong to such as these. If women were generally looked down upon as inferior by the men who made the rules and ran the society, it does not seem at all implausible that Jesus would have associated freely with them and that they would have been particularly intrigued by his proclamation of the coming kingdom.

JESUS, MARY MAGDALENE, AND MARRIAGE151

Some recent scholars have proposed that Jesus in fact did much more than this, that he preached a "radically egalitarian society"— that is, he set about to reform society by inventing a new set of rules to govern social relations, creating a community in which men and women were to be treated as absolute equals.[5] This, however, may be taking the evidence too far and possibly in the wrong direction, for there is little to suggest that Jesus was concerned with pushing social reform in any fundamental way in this evil age. In his view, present-day society and all its conventions were soon to come to a screeching halt, when the Son of Man arrived from heaven in judgment on the earth. Far from transforming society from within, Jesus was preparing people for the destruction of society. Only when God's kingdom arrived would an entirely new order appear, in which peace, equality, and justice would reign supreme. This kingdom, though, would not arrive through the implementation of new social reform programs. It would arrive with a cosmic judge, the Son of Man, who would overthrow the evil and oppressive forces of this world.

To this extent (and I would stress, *only* to this extent), even though Jesus did not urge a social revolution in his time, his message did have radically revolutionary implications. He may have urged his followers to implement these implications in the present (hence his association with women). And in any event, it should be clear that some persons would find his message more attractive than others—especially those who considered themselves downtrodden and oppressed in the present age, who would be rewarded in the age to come. If there were women who felt this way, given the patriarchal structures of their society, small wonder they would have been attracted to the apocalyptic message of Jesus and the hope it held out for life in the kingdom that was coming.

Painting of a
Christian woman
in prayer, from the
Catacomb of
Priscilla.

Was Jesus Married?

We can now turn to the thorny question of whether Jesus himself was married. In *The Da Vinci Code* there is no question about the matter, as both Robert Langdon and Leigh Teabing speak of Jesus' marital status.

As Teabing says at one point to Sophie Neveu:

> "Jesus as a married man makes infinitely more sense than our standard biblical view of Jesus as a bachelor."
> "Why?" Sophie asked.
> "Because Jesus was a Jew," Langdon said. . . . "According to Jewish custom, celibacy was condemned, and the obligation for a Jewish father was to find a suitable wife for his son. If Jesus were

not married, at least one of the Bible's gospels would have mentioned it and offered some explanation for His unnatural state of bachelorhood." (p. 245)

Once again, however, we appear to be in the realm of sensationalized fictional claims instead of the realm of historical reality. I will be dealing in a moment with the general question of whether Jewish men were always married and whether celibacy was "condemned." But first, what have historians said about Jesus' marital status?

It is true that there have occasionally been historical scholars (as opposed to novelists or "independent researchers") who have claimed that it is likely that Jesus was married.[6] But the vast majority of scholars of the New Testament and early Christianity have reached just the opposite conclusion. This is for a variety of compelling reasons.

Most significant is a fact that cannot be overlooked or underestimated: in *none* of our early Christian sources is there any reference to Jesus' marriage or to his wife. This is true not only of the canonical Gospels of Matthew, Mark, Luke, and John but of all our other Gospels and all of our other early Christian writings put together. There is no allusion to Jesus as married in the writings of Paul, the Gospel of Peter, the Gospel of Philip, the Gospel of Mary, the Gospel of the Nazarenes, the Gospel of the Egyptians, the Gospel of the Ebionites—and on and on. List every ancient source we have for the historical Jesus, and in none of them is there mention of Jesus being married.

And just think of all the occasions each of the authors of these books would have had to mention Jesus' marriage or his wife, had he been married. Jesus' mother is mentioned in these books, as are his "father" (Joseph), brothers, and sisters. Why would his wife never be mentioned? His disciples are mentioned; his other followers (including other women) are mentioned. Why would his wife never be? Moreover, the spouses of his followers are occasionally alluded to. And in one passage there is a reference to the wives of the apostles and to the wives of Jesus' earthly brothers (1 Cor. 9:5). Why not to the wife of Jesus? (That this is not just an argument from silence will become clear in a moment.)

More specifically with reference to Mary Magdalene, if Jesus were actually married to her, why would there be no reference to it? Why is she not singled out as special anywhere in the canonical Gospels? Why in fact, apart from Luke 8:1–3, where she is mentioned by name along with two other named women (Joanna and Susanna) and several others, is she not mentioned during his ministry at all, let alone as one who stood in a special relationship with Jesus? Why does she figure in none of the stories about Jesus in these Gospels? And even in Gospels where she is thought of as someone special, such as the Gospel of Mary, why is it as someone to whom Jesus delivered an important revelation, rather than as someone to whom he was married?

More telling still, why is she identified as she is, as Mary Magdalene? Scholars are widely agreed that she is called Magdalene to differentiate her from the other Marys named in the New Testament, including Mary the mother of Jesus and Mary of Bethany, the sister of Martha and Lazarus. *Magdalene* indicates her place of origin—the town of Magdala, a fishing village on the shore of the Sea of Galilee. If one wanted to differentiate this Mary from other Marys, why not indicate that this is the one to whom Jesus was married, rather than to say where she was from? Moreover, if they were married, how is it that Jesus is never portrayed as leaving his hometown until his public ministry, but this woman actually comes from a *different* town (Magdala, rather than Nazareth)?

These are imponderable difficulties for most scholars considering the question of whether Jesus was married, let alone married to Mary Magdalene. She simply doesn't figure prominently in any of our earliest traditions of Jesus, except at the very end, when she along with other women come to anoint his body for burial. And as I pointed out, not even the later Gospels, such as the Gospel of Philip, indicate that they were married (more on these Gospels in the next chapter).

But if in fact Jesus was not married, how can we explain that he was not? Is Robert Langdon right to say that Jewish men were *expected* to be married and that celibacy was "condemned"?

Unfortunately, this again is simply part of the narrative fiction of *The Da Vinci Code*; it has no basis in historical reality (or, perhaps, is based on a tendentious reading of much later Jewish sources). For we do know of Jewish men from the time and place of Jesus who were single, and it is quite clear that they were not "condemned" for it. And what is striking is that this tradition of remaining single and celibate can be found in precisely the same ideological circles as Jesus himself, among Jewish apocalypticists of the first century who expected that the world they lived in soon was to come to a crashing halt when God intervened in history in order to overthrow the forces of evil and bring in his good kingdom.

We know about one group of Jewish apocalypticists in particular from this time and place, as we have already seen. This is the group of Essenes who produced the Dead Sea Scrolls. As it turns out, according to ancient records of these Essenes, they were predominantly single, celibate men. This is the testimony of Jewish sources from the time, such as the first-century philosopher Philo, who indicates that "no Essene takes a wife," and the historian Josephus, who indicates that the Essenes shunned marriage; on the other hand, this view is affirmed even by non-Jewish sources, such as the writings of the Roman polymath Pliny the elder, who indicates that the Essenes renounced sex and lived "without any woman."[7]

Scholars today do not think that Jesus himself was an Essene. But he did have a strikingly similar apocalyptic worldview. That he too would have been unmarried is therefore far from surprising. And in fact his own teachings provide us with grounds for thinking he was unmarried. At one point in our early Gospel accounts Jesus is confronted by a group of Jewish leaders called the Sadducees, who did not believe in an afterlife in the coming kingdom but maintained that death brought total annihilation. Jesus tries to convince them that they are wrong, that there will be an ongoing life for those who are now alive, and even for those who have already died, once the kingdom arrives. But, he insists, that life will differ in at least one significant respect from life in the present, for in the age to come people "neither marry nor are given in marriage, but are like angels in heaven" (Mark 12:25).

But what does this resurrection existence have to do with life in the present? Isn't this simply a description of how things *will* be in the future kingdom? What is worth emphasizing is that a good deal of Jesus' proclamation included his insistence that the ideals of the kingdom should begin to be implemented in the here and now. There will be no hatred then, so people should love one another now; there will be no suffering then, so people should work to alleviate suffering now; there will be no hunger then, so people should feed the hungry now; there will be no war then, so people should work for peace now; there will be no forces of evil then, so people should oppose evil (e.g., by casting out demons) now; there will be no illness then, so people should heal the sick now. That is why Jesus saw the kingdom of God as a "mustard seed," which is planted as a tiny seed now but is to become a huge plant once it grows to full potential (see Mark 4:30–32). The kingdom is like that because it has a small, inauspicious beginning now, as people begin to implement the standards of the kingdom in their lives, but once the Son of Man comes in judgment on the earth to overthrow the forces of evil and bring in God's kingdom, then this small beginning will have a huge result, as the kingdom becomes manifest in power.

Jesus believed that the ideals of the kingdom should be realized in the present. And he believed that in the kingdom there would be no marriage and no sexual relations. This was evidently believed by the Essenes as well, his fellow apocalypticists. They implemented this vision by remaining celibate and unmarried. And it is entirely plausible—indeed likely—that Jesus did the same.

Further evidence comes in the writings of Jesus' followers after his death. The earliest Christian author we have is the apostle Paul, who was not one of Jesus' twelve disciples but was a leader of the movement founded in his name after his death. Like Jesus (and the Essenes before him), Paul too started out as a Jewish apocalypticist. And once he converted to faith in Christ, he did not renounce his apocalyptic worldview but transformed it in view of his belief that the end of the age had already begun with the death and resurrection of Jesus. Paul expected that he himself would be alive when Jesus came back from heaven in judgment on the earth to bring in God's kingdom (see 1 Thess. 4:13–18; 1 Cor. 15:50–57)—he was, in other words, a *Christian* apocalypticist.

And what was his view of marriage? Strikingly, it appears to have been comparable to the view of Jesus himself, that in light of the imminent end, one should devote oneself completely to the coming of the kingdom rather than become married and involved in sexual relationships. In giving advice about marriage and sexual relations to his fellow Christians in the city of Corinth, Paul says: "To those of you who are unmarried, and the widows I say that it is a good thing for them to remain unmarried, just as I am" (1 Cor. 7:8). And why is that? For Paul it was "because of the impending crisis" (1 Cor. 7:26)—in other words, the imminent end of all things. And so those who were married were not to seek a divorce, and those who were unmarried were not to seek to become married (7:27). Instead all people were to commit themselves to converting others to faith in Jesus, to prepare them for the coming destruction of the present social order and the appearance of the kingdom of God, a kingdom in which, according to Jesus, "there is neither marriage nor giving in marriage."

In view of Jesus' apocalyptic message, then, it is not at all surprising that he remained unmarried and celibate. That was explicitly the stand taken by the apocalyptically minded Essenes in his own day, and by his apocalyptically minded follower Paul after his death. Given the fact there is no record at all of Jesus' being married, let alone married to Mary Magdalene, it seems reasonably clear that Jesus the apocalypticist remained single.

Jesus and Mary Magdalene

In light of the circumstance that Jesus probably remained single and celibate, what can we say about his relationship with Mary Magdalene? A lot has been made of this relationship over the years, not simply in novels such as *The Da Vinci Code* and sensationalist works such as *Holy Blood, Holy Grail*, but also in films such as Scorsese's *Last Temptation of Christ* (itself based on the novel by Kazantzakis), where Jesus again is shown to marry Mary Magdalene, a prostitute, and to have had regular sexual relations with her. This view that Jesus had an especially close relationship with Mary has its ancient roots in some of our second- and third-century sources, such as the Gospels of Philip and Mary, which I have already mentioned and which I will discuss at greater length in the following chapter (though I should emphasize that even in these sources Jesus is never said to be married to Mary or to have had sex with her). But here I am interested in the *historical* situation, as this can be discerned not in these later legendary accounts but in our earliest surviving sources. What do we know of Mary Magdalene from them?

As I have indicated, Mary does not in fact appear very often in the Gospel traditions about Jesus: her name is given just thirteen times in the Gospels of the New Testament (as opposed, for example, to Peter's name, which occurs over ninety times), and often these are in parallel passages (e.g., where both Matthew and Mark say the same thing about her in a story that Matthew borrowed from Mark). If we are looking for stories found independently in more than one source, on the assumption that multiply attested traditions are more likely authentic, we can say the following things about Mary. The name Magdalene, as I pointed out, is used to differentiate her from other Marys, including Jesus' mother and his acquaintance Mary of Bethany (sister of Martha). She is said in two separate accounts to have accompanied Jesus on his travels in Galilee (Mark 15:41; Luke 8:1–3), and to have provided funds for his itinerant ministry out of her own pocket (along with other women, some of them left unnamed). All three of our earliest Gospels, Matthew, Mark, and Luke, indicate that she came (together with other women) with Jesus to Jerusalem in the last week of his life, and saw him crucified and buried (Matt. 27:56, 61; Mark 15:40, 47; Luke 23:55). And all four of our canonical Gospels, and the Gospel of

Peter, indicate that it was she who discovered Jesus' empty tomb and learned, either from a man who was there, an angel who was there, or two angels who were there—depending on which account you read—that he had been raised. In one of the accounts she alone learns this (Gospel of John), in the others it is in the company of other women, some of whom are sometimes named. She (and the others) then testified to the empty tomb and are, as such, the first witnesses to the resurrection. In some of the accounts Jesus actually appears to her before he appears to the disciples, after his resurrection.

And that, I'm afraid, is about all that we can find in multiply attested traditions about her. It is easy to wish that there were more information, and there is always the temptation to *invent* more when none is available (Jesus married her! Jesus had sex with her! Jesus had a child with her!). But historians can only go on the basis of the evidence there is, and they shouldn't make up historical evidence when none exists. There is no evidence to suggest that she was "from the Tribe of Benjamin" (as Leigh Teabing claims), and even if she were, this would not make her related to royalty (lots of people came from the tribe of Benjamin, including the apostle Paul; Phil. 3:5); there is nothing to suggest that Jesus entrusted the mission of his church to her (not even the Gospel of Mary indicates this), that he married her, that he had sex with her, or that she ever traveled to France.

There are other references to Mary Magdalene that occur in only one source. Luke, for example, is alone in saying that Jesus had cast "seven demons" out of her. Unfortunately, we don't know what the nature of her demonic possession was, assuming that Luke is right. The idea that these demons drove her to prostitution is a bit far-fetched; most demons in the Gospels prevent people from speaking, or make them ill, or try to harm them by throwing them into fires or lakes. Moreover, there is nothing in any of these references—even the one in Luke—to indicate that Mary even was a prostitute. That idea came about 500 years after these sources were written, when Pope Gregory the Great delivered a sermon in which he indicated that Mary Magdalene was none other than the woman of ill repute mentioned in Luke 7:36–50. But scholars of the Gospels today do not find this iden-tification credible. The story in Luke 7 is about Jesus being anointed by an unnamed woman and is a story that Luke has taken from Mark and jazzed up a bit for his audience. In Mark the woman is not identified as Mary Magdalene and is not, in fact, called there a woman of dubious reputation. In Luke as well the woman does not appear to be Mary Magdalene, since the latter is mentioned in the very next story and Luke *introduces* her there as if for the first time (Luke 8:2). Interestingly, the Gospel of John has a similar story of Jesus' anointing (although it takes place in Bethany of Judea rather than in Galilee, as in Luke); as I have pointed out, though, in John it is Mary of Bethany, not an unnamed woman (or Mary of Magdala) who does the anointing, and she does it in her own home, rather than (as in Luke) at the home of a man named Simon, the Pharisee. In any event, Mary of Bethany and Mary Magdalene come from different towns and are not to be identified as the same person.

Conclusion

In short, we do not learn much about Mary Magdalene in our earliest, most historically reliable sources. No wonder that the curiosity-driven Christians of the second and third centuries who expanded, revised, altered, and sometimes made up traditions about Jesus applied their creative imaginations to this one named woman from Jesus' public ministry and started saying other, nonhistorical things about her. And no wonder these invented stories have resonated with modern readers, who have wanted to know more about Mary Magdalene than can be known. And no wonder, then, that modern legends have been invented about her, including the legend that she was actually married to Jesus, had a normal sexual relationship with him, and bore him a child, the legend found in *Holy Blood, Holy Grail* and taken over virtually unchanged in *The Da Vinci Code*.

Chapter Eight

The Feminine in Early Christianity

One of the key issues raised in *The Da Vinci Code* involves the role of the feminine in Christianity. According to both Leigh Teabing and Robert Langdon, the secret society known as the Priory of Sion has rightly understood that Christianity was originally a religion that celebrated the feminine—both the feminine human and the feminine divine—and incorporated practices into its worship that gave witness to this celebration. This view becomes clear in one of Langdon's early explanations to Sophie Neveu of the distinctive nature of the practice of worship continued by the Priory of Sion in the present day:

> "Sophie," Langdon said, "The Priory's tradition of perpetuating goddess worship is based on a belief that powerful men in the early Christian church 'conned' the world by propagating lies that devalued the female and tipped the scales in favor of the masculine. . . . The Priory believes that Constantine and his male successors successfully converted the world from matriarchal paganism to patriarchal Christianity by waging a campaign of propaganda that demonized the sacred feminine, obliterating the goddess from modern religion forever." (p. 124)

Later in the novel we discover that one of the ways the Priory continues the ancient practice of goddess worship is through the ritual known as *hieros gamos*—literally "sacred marriage"—in which participants observe a male and female leader of the group engage in the sacred act of sex. Sophie herself unwittingly and disastrously observed this mysterious ritual ten years earlier, seeing her own grandfather, Jacques Saunière, curator of the Louvre, engage in the sex act surrounded by robed, masked, and chanting men and women in the basement of their country home. Not knowing what the ritual was, she assumed the worst and broke off all communication with him ever since. What she learns from Robert Langdon and Leigh Teabing, however, is that what she observed was not some kind of kinky sex cult, but a sacred mystery being celebrated by those who understood the true principle of the feminine and the need for the masculine and feminine to be united in order to realize the true divine in nature.

Langdon and Teabing claim that this ritual has ancient roots and that in fact earliest Christianity was invested in understanding and celebrating the feminine principle—that it was only with the interference of the patriarchal emperor Constantine in the fourth century that the feminine came to be demonized in Christianity and women thereby became downgraded, while the masculine, both in humans and in the divinity, was made completely dominant and sacred.

Is this an accurate portrayal of pre-Constantinian Christianity? Were women given exalted roles in the earlier Christian church? Did men and women celebrate the divine principle and worship the feminine aspect of the deity? Did this involve secret sex rituals? Was the feminine principle demonized by Constantine and his male cohorts in the religion?

It is difficult to answer some of these questions. We might begin by considering the practical issue of whether women were
accorded a significant place in the Christian tradition in its early
years, and whether they continued to have positions of prominence (and even power) up to the time of the emperor Constantine.

Women in Early Christianity

It is true that women appear to have played a more prominent
role in the early Christian church than in society at large. We
have already seen that Jesus himself had extensive involvements
with women. There were women, including Mary Magdalene,
who supported his itinerant preaching ministry through their
own funds. Jesus had public discussions and disagreements with
women. He healed women in public. He had women followers,
some of whom accompanied him and his male disciples from
Galilee to Jerusalem in the last week of his life. Women evidently saw him crucified when the male disciples fled the scene;
they saw him buried. And according to all of our earliest traditions, women were the ones who found his tomb empty on the
third day and began the proclamation that he had been raised
from the dead. All in all, women played a significant role in the
life and death of Jesus.

What about in the churches established in his name after his
death? It is true that just as men played the most prominent
roles during Jesus' lifetime, so too they did after his death. The
leaders of the original Christian community in Jerusalem appear to have been the core members of his (male) apostolic
band—especially the apostle Peter—along with one of Jesus'
brothers, James, who evidently converted to faith in Jesus soon

after the crucifixion (1 Cor. 15:7). Men were put in charge of the practical arrangements of the church (Acts 6). Most of the early Christian missionaries known from such sources as the Acts of the Apostles were men—people such as Barnabas, Philip, and the newly converted Paul of Tarsus (Acts 8–9). Many of the most important converts to the faith are said to have been men, such as the Roman centurion Cornelius (Acts 10–11). At the conference called to deal with the central problem confronting the new church—whether non-Jewish converts needed to observe the Jewish Law in order to be followers of Jesus—the principal speakers were all men (Acts 15). And so on.

Could this male orientation be chalked up to the biases of the author of Acts, rather than to the historical realities of the case? Probably not: this author, who also wrote the Gospel of Luke, is well known for emphasizing the role of women in the life of Jesus himself, more so than the writers of our other Gospels. So perhaps his portrayal in Acts is accurate (or at least not overt patriarchal propaganda). There are nonetheless counterindications to suggest that women did play a significant role in the burgeoning Christian communities of the first century. This evidence comes from the writings of the apostle Paul, our earliest Christian author, who wrote a number of letters to churches in order to discuss their various problems and to help them resolve them. Throughout Paul's letters it is clear that women, while not as prominent in the communities as men, occasionally had positions of preeminence and power.

Women in the Churches of Paul

The best evidence comes in Paul's letter to the Romans.[1] Here Paul greets a number of members of the congregation by name, and it is striking that women feature prominently in these greetings. Although Paul names more men than women, the women in the church appear to be in no way inferior to their male counterparts. Paul names Phoebe, a deacon (or minister) in the church of Cenchreae and Paul's own patron, to whom he entrusted the delivery of the letter to the Romans (16:1–2). He mentions Prisca, who along with her husband, Aquila, is largely responsible for the Gentile mission and who supports a congregation in her home (vv. 3–4; notice that she is named ahead of her husband). He greets Mary, his colleague who works among the Romans (v. 6). He names Tryphaena, Tryphosa, and Persis, women whom Paul calls his "co-workers" for the gospel (vv.; 6, 12). And he speaks of Julia and the mother of Rufus and the sister of Nereus, all of whom appear to have a high profile in this community (vv. 13, 15). Most impressively of all, he mentions Junia, whom he calls "foremost among the apostles" (v. 7). The apostolic band was evidently larger and more inclusive than the list of twelve men most people know about.

Others of Paul's letters provide a similar impression of women's active involvement in the Christian churches. For example, in his letter to the Corinthians we learn of women who actively participate in the worship services by using their "spiritual gifts," which, among other things, allow them to utter divinely inspired prophecies to the congregation (1 Cor. 11:4–6). And in Philippians the only two members of the congregation that Paul calls by name are two women, Euodia and Syntyche, whose dissension causes the apostle some concern, apparently because of their prominent standing in the community (Phil. 4:2).

If Christianity were a strictly male-oriented religion, as some people have maintained, it would be difficult to explain the prominent roles women appear to have had in Paul's churches. But how do we explain the situation in light of Paul's actual teachings about men and women? In the case of Jesus we have seen that it was probably his apocalyptic message that attracted women to be his followers: in the coming kingdom there would be a reversal of fortunes, where the downtrodden and oppressed were to be exalted to positions of power. Women could naturally find a message of hope in this proclamation—especially those who kept under the thumb of their male family members in ancient patriarchal societies. As we have seen, Paul too was an apocalypticist. Could that also explain the important roles played by women in his churches, that they were in some sense already implementing the ideals of the kingdom in the here and now, reversing the patriarchal assumptions of their society and playing a role equal to that of men in the smaller social settings of the churches?

A key verse for understanding Paul's view of women is Galatians 3:28, where he states that every Christian who has been "baptized into Christ" has already begun to experience the freedoms from social distinctions of the present age: "There is no longer Jew or Greek, there is no longer slave or free, there is no longer male and female; for you are all one in Christ Jesus." Based on this verse, one would expect there to be no distinctions in the Christian communities based on social standing or social status: all people are equal "in Christ." And yet it is also clear from Paul's other writings that he, like Jesus, never urged a social revolution in which the distinctions of this world were to be done away with in bringing in a better society. Paul never, for example, urges the abolition of slavery; he instead assumes that it will continue as a social institution in this world (see his letter to Philemon). And although "in Christ . . . there is not male and female," the reality is that people, including Christians, continue to live in this world until the kingdom comes. So even though Paul urged that ultimately there will be no distinction between genders, in the present this distinction continues to exist.

That is why Paul can tell the women in Corinth that when they pray and prophesy in church, they must do so while wearing their veils (1 Cor. 11:2–16). Some women of the congregation had evidently taken him seriously when he argued that in Christ there were no gender distinctions, and they began speaking publicly without having their heads covered (a social faux pas for women at the time). Paul insisted on the contrary that the distinctions *do* continue to exist in the present, even if eventually they will be done away with. And so women should not dress or behave like men; they should have head coverings (whereas men should not).

Women in the Post-Pauline Churches

Paul's position on women may strike modern readers as highly ambivalent at best: women and men are theoretically equal in Christ, but not really. Men should behave as men and women as women. It is striking that after Paul's day, different leaders of his churches stressed one or the other side of this ambivalent position. We know of some later Pauline Christians, for example, who stressed the equality of women, who insisted that women should be as active as men in the Christian churches and the Christian mission. Nowhere can this be seen more clearly than in the legendary tales surrounding an alleged female disciple of Paul's named Thecla.

The stories about Thecla were in wide circulation in the second and third Christian centuries.[2] In them we learn that Thecla was a pagan woman, engaged to be married, who happens one day to hear the proclamation of the apostle Paul. This proclamation, according to the tale, is that all people, men and women, are to live lives of complete chastity. Those who are married are not to engage in sex; those who are unmarried should remain unmarried. By being chaste, a person can inherit the kingdom of God.

Thecla takes this teaching to heart and breaks off her engagement, much to the chagrin and anger of her former fiancé, who out of bitterness turns her over to the Roman authorities as a Christian deserving punishment. In a series of intriguing and exciting episodes, Thecla is supernaturally protected from harm when thrown to the wild beasts and when nearly burned at the stake. She eventually manages to join up with Paul and becomes a lifelong advocate of his teaching of chastity, herself going on a Christian mission to spread this good news and to convert others to the faith of Paul.

It is difficult to know how much historical credence can be given to any of these stories, but clearly they struck a resonant note with many readers. Some scholars think that the readership may, in fact, have been predominantly women, for the life of chastity could be seen as a life of freedom—freedom from confines of patriarchal marriages in which a woman was subject to the will and whims of her husband. Commitment to the gospel of Paul, therefore, could well be a liberating experience in a world of male dominance. Certainly there were numerous Christians of the second and third centuries who saw Paul as one committed to this kind of liberation for women.

But there were other Christians who saw Paul in just the opposite light, as one who endorsed the subservience of women both in their marriages and in the church. This view of Paul can be seen already within the writings of the New Testament itself. I have mentioned before that there are thirteen letters that go under Paul's name in the New Testament. But since the nineteenth century scholars have put forth compelling reasons for thinking that some of these letters were actually written not by Paul but by later followers in Paul's name. In particular, there is a wide scholarly consensus that Paul did not write the "Pastoral" epistles of 1 and 2 Timothy and Titus.[3] What is striking is that these books take just the opposite view of Paul from that found in the tales of his alleged female convert Thecla. For here it is men who are to be in charge of the churches; women are to be subservient to men in every way. In probably the most notorious passage of these epistles, "Paul" (i.e., the pseudonymous author writing in Paul's name) says the following:

> Let a woman learn in silence in full submission. I do not allow a woman to teach or to exercise authority over a man; they should be silent. For Adam was made first, and then Eve. And Adam did not go astray, but the woman went astray and entered into transgression. But she will be saved through bearing children, if they remain in faith and love and holiness, with modesty. (1 Tim. 2:11–15)

In the letters that Paul himself actually wrote, as well as in the later, legendary Acts of Thecla, we find accounts of women actively engaged in church ministry: praying, prophesying, and teaching (and in later traditions, such as Thecla's, baptizing). But according to this passage in 1 Timothy, all that is forbidden. Women are to be completely silent and submissive; their salvation comes only by producing children.[4]

I should point out two salient issues here: (1) this is the view that eventually won out in the struggles between women who wanted a more prominent place in the Christian community and men (and arguably women) who wanted women to be subordinate to men, and (2) this restriction of the roles of women did not first occur with the emperor Constantine but was already in place centuries before. It is a view that is already found in the writings of the New Testament itself.

But how did we get from the Paul of Galatians 3:28, who maintained that in Christ there is gender equality, to the "Paul" of the Pastoral epistles, who insisted on male dominance? Many scholars think that it happened like this. In the earliest churches there was an apocalyptic fervor, in which the end of all things was thought to be at hand. In the kingdom that was soon to arrive, there would be complete equality, and that equality should be manifest on some level in the here and now in anticipation of what things would be like then. But the kingdom never did come, and the church settled in for the long haul. That led the Christians to resume their normal lives according to the patterns that were well established in society at large—which meant, among other things, that women were removed from positions of prestige and made subservient to men. The religion became patriarchalized with the passing of time and the nonappearance of the kingdom. This happened relatively quickly, so that in most Christian churches of the second century, women no longer played a significant role. Again, this was not a decision made by Constantine; by his day, the decision was ancient history.

This is not to say that all Christians of the second century rejected the role of women. On the contrary, the stories of Thecla and others like her were popular precisely because there were strong countermovements in some places. I can mention two such places here.

Women in the Montanist Movement

The Montanist movement is named after a late-second-century prophet, Montanus, who predicted that the kingdom of God was soon to appear (the apocalyptic movement within Christianity never did die out completely—it continues on, in fact, to the present day) and who warned Christians that, as a result, they needed to live their lives in preparation, following strict moral principles. Early on Montanus acquired as followers two women prophets named Maximilla and Priscilla, who came to be seen as equally important in the divine utterances that they made, allegedly under the inspiration of the Spirit. These women evidently saw themselves as key figures in the apocalyptic scenario about to unfold. As Maximilla once predicted, "After me there will be no more prophecy, but the End."[5]

One might think that given the centrality of these women to the movement, there would be some kind of equality of the genders evident in Montanist circles. But as it turns out, there is little correlation between the social reality (women prophets) and ideological emphasis (the secondary standing of women). The most famous convert to the Montanist cause was the feisty and prolific Christian apologist, polemicist, and heresy hunter Tertullian of Carthage (160–225 CE), one of the great misogynists of Christian antiquity. Tertullian was avid in his attack on women who believed they could exercise leadership roles in the church; his views of women in general can be seen in the opening of a tractate that he wrote urging women not to adorn themselves in fine garments or with jewelry so as to make themselves attractive (since in fact before God they are not). Here he points out that every woman is a descendant of Eve, and like their forebear each is personally guilty of all the sin that has come into the world to plague man (i.e., males):

> Do you not know that you are each an Eve? The sentence of God on this sex of yours lives in this age: the guilt must of necessity live too. *You* are the devil's gateway: *you* are the unsealer of that forbidden tree: *you* are the first deserter of the divine law:

you are she who persuaded him [i.e., Adam] whom the devil was not valiant enough to attack. *You* destroyed so easily God's image, man. On account of *your* desert—that is death—even the Son of God had to die. And do you think about adorning yourselves?[6]

Not a very liberated view. My point is that even where we can find women in prominent roles in a religion, that does not necessarily mean that women are celebrated for their femininity or that one can find the divine feminine wherever there are prominent women. Sometimes just the opposite is the case.

Women in Gnosticism
In the centuries before Constantine, probably the one branch of Christianity where women featured most prominently was in the various Gnostic religions we have already discussed. I should reemphasize that Gnosticism was not *one* thing—it was lots of different religions that had several key points in common, for example the dualistic belief that this material world was evil and that the spiritual realm was good, and the notion that it was divinely given knowledge (gnosis) that could bring liberation from this evil existence. It does appear, however, that within a number of Gnostic religions women played prominent roles and that the divine feminine was to some extent celebrated. There is even evidence of the celebration of rituals not unlike the *hieros gamos* described in *The Da Vinci Code*. But the evidence is in most cases ambiguous and difficult to interpret.

The opponents of the various Gnostic forms of religion were the church fathers whose works were later declared to be orthodox.[7] These writers sometimes attacked Gnostics for their bizarre (to the orthodox) understanding of the divine realm—which was inhabited not by the one true God, but by numerous gods, both masculine and feminine. Moreover, they attacked Gnostics

on the grounds that women were allowed to exercise prominent, leadership roles in their communities. Even from the surviving Gnostic writings themselves we occasionally get glimpses
of the importance of women and the feminine principle. Some
of these writings, as we have seen, are quoted in *The Da Vinci
Code*, especially two Gospels alluded to earlier, the Gospel of
Mary and the Gospel of Philip. Here we do well to take a closer
look at these writings.

THE GOSPEL OF MARY

The Gospel of Mary was probably composed sometime during
the (late?) second century.[8] Even though we do not have the complete text, it was clearly an intriguing Gospel, for here, among
other things, Mary Magdalene is accorded a high status among
the apostles of Jesus. In fact, at the end of the text, the apostle
Levi acknowledges to his comrades that Jesus "loved her more
than us." Mary's special relationship with Jesus is seen above all in
the circumstance that he reveals to her alone, in a vision, an explanation of the nature of things hidden from the apostles.

The Gospel divides itself into two parts. In the first, Jesus,
after his resurrection, gives a revelation to all his apostles concerning the nature of sin, speaks a final blessing and exhorta-
tion, commissions them to preach the gospel, and then leaves.
They are saddened by his departure, but Mary consoles them
and urges them to reflect on what he has said. She is then asked
by Peter to tell them what Jesus had told her directly. In the
second part of the Gospel, she describes the vision that she had
been granted. Unfortunately, four pages are lost from the manuscript, and so we know only the beginning and end of her description. But it appears that the vision involved a conversation
she had with Jesus, who described how the human soul could

ascend past the four ruling powers of the world in order to find its eternal rest. This description of the fate of the soul is related to salvation narratives found in other Gnostic texts.

The Gospel continues with two of the apostles—Andrew and Peter—challenging Mary's vision and her claim to have experienced it; it ends, though, with Levi pointing out that she was Jesus' favorite and urging them to go forth to preach the gospel as he commanded. They are said to do so, and there the Gospel ends.[9]

Here, then, is a text that highlights the importance of Mary, a woman, as the one to whom Christ has made a special revelation that can bring salvation. I should probably point out that Leigh Teabing completely misrepresents this text in *The Da Vinci Code*, where he says:

> At this point in the gospels, Jesus suspects He will soon be captured and crucified. So He gives Mary Magdalene instructions on how to carry on His church after He is gone. . . . According to these unaltered gospels, it was not *Peter* to whom Christ gave directions with which to establish the Christian Church. It was *Mary Magdalene*. (pp. 247–48)

That in fact is not an accurate description. The discussion recorded in the Gospel of Mary takes place *after* Jesus' crucifixion, not before, and the revelation given to Mary is not about how to carry on his church but about how to find salvation for the soul. Nonetheless, this is at least one Gnostic writing where a woman is given special prominence. At the same time, I should point out that this prominence is not undisputed and unambiguously celebrated. Just the opposite is the case: the book is largely about whether or not Mary's vision can be trusted, since it was given to a woman. Apparently some members of the Gnostic community that produced this text answered this question in one way, and others in another.

THE GOSPEL OF PHILIP

A second Gnostic text that figures most prominently in *The Da Vinci Code* is known as the Gospel of Philip.[10] This book was almost completely unknown until discovered in 1945 as one of the documents in the Nag Hammadi Library. Although it is easily recognized as a Gnostic work, possibly of the early third century, the book is notoriously difficult to understand in its details. In part this is because of how it is composed: it is a collection of mystical reflections that have been excerpted from previously existing sermons, treatises, and theological meditations, brought together here under the name of Jesus' disciple Philip. Since these reflections are given in relative isolation, without any real narrative context, they are difficult to interpret.[11]

One of the clearest emphases of the text is the contrast between those who can understand and those who cannot, between knowledge that is exoteric (available to all) and that which is esoteric (available only to insiders), between the immature outsiders (regular Christians, called "Hebrews") and the mature insiders (Gnostics, called "Gentiles"). Those who do not understand, the outsiders with only exoteric knowledge, err in many of their judgments—for example, in taking such notions as the virgin birth (v. 17) or the resurrection of Jesus (v. 21) as literal statements of historical fact rather than symbolic expressions of deeper truths.

Throughout much of the work the Christian sacraments figure prominently. Five are explicitly named: baptism, anointing, Eucharist, salvation, and bridal chamber (v. 68). It is hard to know what deeper meaning these rituals had for the author. Especially intriguing, however, is the sacrament of the bridal chamber. Is this a reference to some kind of union of masculine and feminine, a ritualized celebration of the sex act entered into by believing members of the community, like the *hieros gamos* of

The Da Vinci Code? Scholars are divided on the question. Given the absence of any explanation of the sacrament in the Gospel itself, the truth is that we really don't know what it was.

There are two passages of the Gospel of Philip that figure prominently in *The Da Vinci Code*. One I have already mentioned:

> "There were three who always walked with the lord: Mary his mother and her sister and the Magdalene, the one who was called his companion. His sister and his mother and his companion were each a Mary."

Leigh Teabing claims that the Aramaic word for "companion" really meant "spouse," and uses this to show that Jesus and Mary Magdalene were married. But as we have seen, the text is written not in Aramaic but in Coptic, and the word for "companion" (it's a Greek loanword, *koinōnos*) in fact means not "spouse" but "companion," "friend," or "associate."

The other passage is even more intriguing, but there is a problem with it that I should mention before quoting it. The manuscript that contains the Gospel of Philip is worn in places, having a number of holes where the words are, therefore, missing. This has affected one passage in particular:

> The companion of the [gap in the manuscript] Mary Magdalene [gap] more than [gap] the disciples [gap] kiss her [gap] on her [gap].

Obviously Christ is kissing Mary somewhere—but where is impossible to say. The text continues on in a vein similar to what can be found in the Gospel of Mary, involving a dispute among the male disciples about why Jesus loves Mary more than them:

> They said to him, "Why do you love her more than all of us?" The savior answered and said to them, "Why do I not love you like her?"

Once again it is clear that there are some who celebrate Christ's love of the woman over that of the men, but it would probably be wrong to see his love for Mary as different in *kind* from his love of his male disciples (i.e., it's not romantic love); it is a difference instead of *degree*.

In any event, it is easy to see why the orthodox church fathers, who were supporters of patriarchal religion and saw God himself as a "father" (not a father and mother, for example), may have understood Gnostics as having gone astray, both in their view that the divine realm was made up of a number of deities, both male and female, and in the importance attached to women in their movement. It is certainly not right to say, however, that these emphases on the feminine were ubiquitous in the Christian movement as a whole before Constantine (the claim of Leigh Teabing and Robert Langdon in *The Da Vinci Code*); they were in one branch of Christianity—several of the multifarious groups that go under the rubric "Gnostic"—and not everywhere in the religion. And these views had come to be marginalized many years before Constantine arrived on the scene. He was not the one responsible for taking the feminine principle in Christianity and demonizing it.

But this takes us to a second set of questions: apart from the disputed role of women in the early Christian churches, do we have evidence that the feminine principle was ever worshiped, or that Christians engaged in the sacred ritual of *hieros gamos*?

The Feminine Principle in Early Christianity

This too is a complicated set of questions to answer, because our sources are so sparse and so ambiguous.

To begin with, there is little to suggest that most Christians in the early centuries were committed to worshiping the divine feminine. Starting with Jesus himself, our earliest records indicate that he saw God as his "father" and worshiped him as such. Just within our earliest Gospels, "father" is a common epithet for God on the lips of Jesus (it occurs forty-five times in the Gospel of Matthew alone, for example); never in these sources does he speak of God as "mother" or "sister" or any other feminine sobriquet. And this should come as no surprise: Jesus was a male Jewish apocalypticist who believed that in the coming kingdom there would be no marriage or sexual activity. Jesus did not celebrate sexual difference because he believed it would eventually be extinguished.

So too with Paul, an author widely favored among Gnostics. Paul believed that in Christ there is no male and female. In his view, in the age to come sex differences would be eliminated. Possibly he thought that in that age, all people would revert to the original state of humans in the beginning, when God created the human but had not yet differentiated the male from the female (which happened only later, when he made Eve out of Adam's rib). In other words, people would be androgynous. Here too there is no celebration of the feminine, but an anticipation of the elimination of the feminine (along with the masculine).

We find a similar emphasis even in Gnostic sources where the feminine is otherwise celebrated more highly—for example, in the Gnostic belief that the divine realm consists of both masculine and feminine deities, and in the notion that the spark of the divine within some humans is in fact a part of the feminine deity Sophia, who has come to be entrapped in this world of matter (see my discussion in chapter 2). But even here there is no consistent praise of the feminine per se. Recall the saying of the Gnostic Gospel of Thomas:

Simon Peter said to them, "Let Mary leave us, for women are not worthy of life."

Jesus said, "I myself shall lead her in order to make her male, so that she too may become a living spirit resembling you males. For every woman who will make herself male will enter the kingdom of heaven." (Gosp. Thom. 114)

Here we have (again) a dispute about the role of women in salvation, but even more we have not a celebration of femininity but an insistence that it must be destroyed: only males can enter the kingdom (see my discussion in chapter 3).

Or consider another saying of Thomas that may echo the sentiments of Paul, that in the end there will be no masculine or feminine, but only one whole human being:

Jesus said to them, "When you make the two one, and when you make the inside like the outside and the outside like the inside . . . and when you make the male and the female one and the same, so that the male not be male nor the female female . . . then you will enter the kingdom." (Gosp. Thom. 22)

Other Gnostic groups no doubt did celebrate the feminine, but scholars are sharply divided on how to read the texts.[12] Does the presence of feminine deities and the high profile of women indicate a celebration of the feminine divine? One should not overlook the evidence from other areas of Christendom, such as Montanism, where a prominent role given to women did not at all lead to a widely held sense of the importance of the feminine.

Ritual Celebrations of the Feminine

Finally, were there ritualistic celebrations of the feminine, for example in ancient equivalents of the *hieros gamos*? We have seen that some such ritual was possibly enacted in the community that produced the Gospel of Philip, where the sacrament of the mysterious "bridal chamber" was celebrated. The most explicit reference to some such ritual, however, does not celebrate the feminine but instead, evidently, degrades it. Unfortunately, this reference needs to be taken with more than a grain of salt, as it occurs in the writing of a fourth-century orthodox church father named Epiphanius, who was intent above all else in attacking "heresies," including those of the Gnostics.

In a lengthy refutation of the practices of one Gnostic group, called the Phibionites (and called by other names as well), Epiphanius details a sex ritual that sounds in some respects very much like what Sophie Neveu witnessed in the basement of her country home.[13] According to Epiphanius, in a secret ritual held at night and only for the insiders of the group, the Phibionites all pair off with someone other than their own spouse and engage in ritual sex; but at the point of climax, the man withdraws from the woman and they collect his semen in their hands. They then consume it together, saying, "This is the body of Christ." When possible, they collect the menstrual blood of the woman as well, and consume it together, saying, "This is the blood of Christ." If the woman inadvertently becomes pregnant (when the attempt at coitus interruptus failed), the fetus is aborted and eaten in a communal meal, which they call the "perfect Passover."

Epiphanius claims that these couples who engage in this sex act do so to replicate the events that transpire in the heavenly realms and thereby enable their own passage back to their heavenly homes, whence they have come, trapped in these mortal bodies. One of the interesting things about this description is that rather than celebrating the feminine, the way the Priory of Sion's ritual allegedly does, this one appears to denigrate it. It is precisely the feminine functions of conception and childbearing that are denied, for the point of the sex act is for the woman *not* to become pregnant, and babies are *not* to be produced. Women's role in the sex act is not therefore focused on what makes them women (other than the fact they have menstrual blood); it is no surprise that Epiphanius goes on to indicate that some of the more highly positioned leaders of the community (these are all men) engage in ritual masturbation so that they can eat the body of Christ in the privacy of their own rooms.

It is very difficult to trust much of what Epiphanius says about this ritual—some scholars doubt whether there is any historical basis for it at all.[14] It is certainly difficult to see where he would have learned the details—these would have been secret rituals for insiders, not for the general public to observe for the price of admission; and even the groups' books (which Epiphanius claims to have read) would not have been how-to manuals. It may be that something like these rituals did take place, or it may be that the description is all from Epiphanius's own fertile, and somewhat voyeuristic, imagination.

Conclusion

It is very difficult for historians to know how to evaluate the role of women and the importance of the "feminine" in early Christianity. Some things, however, we can say for certain. In the beginning of the Christian movement, women played a more prominent role than they did later. They were well represented in the ministry of Jesus himself and in the earliest Christian communities associated with Paul. But eventually patriarchal forces made their power known in Christianity, as evidenced, for example, in the Pastoral epistles, where women are instructed to be subservient to men. Even the scriptural authority of these

instructions, however, did not silence all Christian women everywhere, as can be seen in the tales of Thecla, in the Montanist
movement, and in some of the Gnostic groups of the second and
third centuries.

It is not right to say, however, that wherever women were prominent there was a high evaluation of the feminine, as we saw in
the case of Tertullian and the Montanists. The various groups
of Gnostics are probably where women continued to exercise
the greatest authority, and where the feminine aspect of the divine was celebrated most consistently. But even here there are
question marks concerning whether Gnostics uniformly appre-
ciated the feminine per se, or whether they believed that women
should transcend their femininity, either to become more like
males or to reach the state where there is no difference between
masculine and feminine. In any event, it is not clear how far
these various understandings of the feminine came to be manifest in the worship lives of these communities, and whether there
was any ritualistic celebration of the divine feminine or the feminine principle itself as found in actual women.

One thing that is clear is that Christianity before Constantine
was *not* a matriarchal religion, only to be patriarchalized after the
interference of the Roman emperor. The claims of *The Da Vinci
Code* notwithstanding, patriarchy had triumphed throughout most
of Christianity long before the early fourth century, and Constantine himself had nothing to do with it.

Epilogue

I'd like to end this book in the same way I began, on a personal note. When I arrived at my new teaching position at the University of North Carolina at Chapel Hill in 1988, my first course was a class called "Jesus in Myth, Tradition, and History." As luck would have it, the semester started just as Martin Scorsese's film *The Last Temptation of Christ* was released in the theaters. I wanted to take advantage of the moment by requiring my students to see the film and to write a critique of it, based on what they had learned in class. This kind of requirement would not have been a problem in the Northeast, where I had come from, teaching at Rutgers University in New Jersey. But I was in for a rude awakening teaching in the South, in the buckle of the Bible Belt. There was a small student uprising in protest of my requirement, as several students from conservative religious backgrounds believed it would be sacrilegious for them to see the film. They refused to go and indicated they would rather flunk the course.

I found this a bit hard to believe at the time. These were young adults who should have realized that you can't criticize a film without seeing it, any more than you can criticize a book without reading it or a course without taking it. But they were highly critical of the film and refused. I ended up rescinding the requirement (thinking that forcing them to do something that violated their religious convictions was probably an infringement of some constitutional right or other) and instead made it a voluntary affair: students could come with me to see the film if they liked, and afterward we would discuss it over pizza.

As it turns out, I didn't like the film much on that first viewing (I have since liked it more and more every time I've seen it). Many of my students didn't like it either. For them the problem was the sexual relationship between Jesus and Mary Magdalene (played by Willem Dafoe and Barbara Hershey, respectively; I still think her Magdalene is the best ever), which they thought went way too far. That didn't bother me so much—not because I think Jesus and Mary actually did have sex, but because it was all part of the fictional makeup of the movie, and I thought that was okay. What did bother me was the overall portrayal of Jesus as someone who couldn't make up his mind about who he was, one time thinking he was the messiah, another time that he was the Son of Man, another time that he was the Son of God, and so forth and so on. That just seemed to me to be a cheap way of saying that Scorsese (or Kazantzakis, who wrote the novel) couldn't decide who Jesus was, and so put his own uncertainties onto the shoulders of the character. I guess I had an uneasy feeling that people seeing the film would decide Jesus really was like that—completely fickle about his character—whereas I saw him quite differently, as someone who knew full well who he was from the outset.

At the time I was reminded of my reaction to the Monty Python film *The Life of Brian* when it first came out. I thought parts of it were outrageously funny—although I have to admit that I felt terrifically guilty laughing at the final crucifixion scene, where hanging on their crosses they all break out into the song, "Always Look on the Bright Side of Life." But I felt even more disturbed by the portrayal of first-century Palestine as being chock-full of Jewish apocalyptic crazies, all predicting this, that, or the other scenario for the coming end of the world. I remember thinking that people who saw the movie might think that that's how it really was, and again the "historical" understanding of Jesus might be affected by it.

I suppose I'm older and wiser now, because I like *The Last Temptation of Christ* and *The Life of Brian* almost without reserve these days, and show them to students on occasion (for some reason I get fewer protests now). But I was put off, again, just a couple of months ago by Mel Gibson's *The Passion of the Christ*, and for much the same reason. The basic message transposed onto Jesus struck me as offensive. In this case it was something like "More pain, more gain": people have a lot of sins to atone for, so Jesus goes at it with full vigor, being beaten to a bloody pulp before our very eyes. And why? Because that's just what he had to do. His pain is our gain. This strikes me as at odds with how the Gospels portray Jesus' last hours, and I can't help but find the message a bit repulsive. Still, I suppose eventually I might mellow out about that movie as well.

I have come to see in each of these instances that for some reason or another I am concerned that people not get the wrong impression about the past from a cinematic portrayal of it. Maybe this is just one of my quirks as a historian. But the reality is that historical movies *are* one of the chief ways people come to think about the past. I have to confess that even though I am supposed to have as one of my areas of expertise the events of the early

Roman Empire, I enjoyed very much (and learned some things from) the BBC broadcast of *I Claudius*. And I learned some things about the Roman republic in the days of Marius, Sulla, and Julius Caesar from the novels of Colleen McCullough (*First Man in Rome*, etc.). Although I am a historian by profession, even my own views of the past are affected by the films I see and the books I read. How much more must this be true for people who do other things with their lives, who only occasionally come in contact with events from the ancient world, usually not through the work of historians and scholars of antiquity, but through books and film.

I sometimes have to remind myself that we historians are a strange lot. We learn several dead languages (my case is typical: Greek, Latin, Syriac, Hebrew, Coptic); we study texts such as the writings of the New Testament or the works of the early church fathers in intricate detail; we spend countless hours reading scholarship produced by other historians on these documents. Obviously most people aren't like that. At best most people have a mild interest in the world of antiquity, and their interest is not seriously piqued except through a powerful movie or a page-turning novel.

The Da Vinci Code, more than any other book of recent memory, has really done the trick. The story itself is fast-paced, intricate, compelling, spellbinding. And the historical moments in which the past—especially Christian antiquity—is discussed are integrated so well into the fiction that it seems to take almost no effort at all to pick up information about Jesus, Mary Magdalene, the emperor Constantine, the formation of the Christian Bible, and the noncanonical gospels. What a terrific way to learn history—completely painless!

The problem is that people who read a book like this have no way of separating the historical fact from the literary fiction. The author himself won't help you out by telling you which historical claims are just as fictional as the characters and the plot of the novel. And in many places, he himself may not know. He's a novelist, not a scholar of history.

And so, to return to my starting point, that's why I wanted to write this book. It was not simply to correct the mistakes and then give Dan Brown a grade on how well he did. It was not because I was afraid religious people might experience a rupture in their faith unless someone set the record straight. And it certainly was not to castigate the book as a work of fiction. I really like it as a work of fiction and have recommended it to my friends (as have about eight million other people).

My objective in fact has been somewhat more modest. *The Da Vinci Code* has so well succeeded where professional historians have miserably failed: it has gotten people interested in a range of historical questions about early Christianity. These are things that I too am interested in. And talking about *The Da Vinci Code* has made it possible for me to talk about these things. One of the reasons I'm interested in them is because, well, they are interesting. For some people it takes a *Da Vinci Code* to see what can be interesting in the past, not just for the dull professorial types who read dead languages for a living but for average people who might find it interesting to know something about Jesus, or Mary Magdalene, or the emperor Constantine, or about how we came to get the books we call the New Testament.

If Dan Brown had gotten all his facts straight, there would have been no compelling reason for me to write this book. But he didn't. Some people may think that he can (and should) be blamed for the historical mistakes: it would not have taken that

much homework (a few hours, maybe) to learn that the Dead
Sea Scrolls didn't contain any Christian documents, or that the
Gospel of Philip is not in Aramaic, or that there were not thousands of documents from Jesus' own day recording his activities.
But on the other hand, I have to keep emphasizing that Dan
Brown was writing *fiction*. Even though he claims that his "descriptions of . . . documents . . . are accurate," in fact they are
not. That too, as it turns out, is part of the fiction. In some ways,
recognizing that point can make the fiction more enjoyable as
creative, imaginative, and (some might think) less accountable
to the truth of history as it really happened. But it can also open
up doors for people interested in knowing about the past, based
not on a fictional account of the search for the Grail but on the
historical record.

And for some of us the historical record really does matter,
possibly because in some ways, history is like any other good
story. It is a narrative that we tell and retell, filled with characters that we can relate to, with plots and subplots that we some-
how feel a part of. The past is a story that we ourselves can live
in, one that can inform our lives in the present. It is a true story,
one that contributes to our sense of ourselves and our place in
the world. And for that reason, if for no other, it seems important for us to know the truth about what happened in the past.
As it turns out, this is a view of history that is shared by the
characters of *The Da Vinci Code*. All the more reason to know
whether their version of the past is historically accurate or not,
whether their historical claims are true or flights of literary fancy.

Notes

Chapter One

1. For further information on early Christian persecution, see Bart D. Ehrman, *After the New Testament: A Reader in Early Christianity* (New York: Oxford University Press, 1999), chap. 3; and Bart D. Ehrman and Andrew S. Jacobs, *Christianity in Late Antiquity 300–450 C.E.: A Reader* (New York: Oxford University Press, 2004), chap. 2.

2. Jews also did not worship the pagan gods, of course, but Jews were treated as an acceptable exception, since they had such an ancient and venerable form of worship and did not impinge on the worship of the gods by others.

3. For this account, see Ehrman and Jacobs, *Christianity in Late Antiquity*, pp. 30–43.

4. James Carroll, *Constantine's Sword: The Church and the Jews* (Boston: Houghton Mifflin, 2001), p. 171.

5. Mark himself may not have thought that as "Son of God," Jesus was himself divine. But that was certainly how Mark was *understood* in later centuries. See Bart D. Ehrman, *The New Testament: A Historical Introduction to the Early Christian Writings*, 3rd ed. (New York: Oxford University Press, 2004), pp. 69–70.

6. See Ehrman and Jacobs, *Christianity in Late Antiquity*, pp. 155–66.

7. See Ehrman and Jacobs, *Christianity in Late Antiquity*, pp. 251–55.

Chapter Two

1. For Leigh Teabing, of course, Mary Magdalene is the "Grail," and the Nag Hammadi Library *does* speak of her. But it never speaks of her as the one who contained Jesus' seed. And she is never mentioned in the Dead Sea Scrolls.

2. For a very useful digest of information on the Dead Sea Scrolls, see Joseph A. Fitzmyer, *Responses to 101 Questions on the Dead Sea Scrolls* (New York: Paulist Press, 1982). The most recent reliable survey is by James Vanderkam, *The Meaning of the Dead Sea Scrolls: Their Significance for Understanding the Bible, Judaism, Jesus, and Christianity* (San Francisco: HarperSanFrancisco, 2002). On the archaeological questions, see Jodi Magness, *The Archaeology of Qumran and the Dead Sea Scrolls* (Grand Rapids: Eerdmans, 2002).

3. Some scholars have claimed that there were fragments of New Testament documents among the documents discovered in Cave 7, but they have failed to convince almost all the experts. See Fitzmyer, *101 Questions*, pp. 16, 104–10.

4. I have taken this account, with only minor editorial changes, from my book *Lost Christianities: The Battles for Scripture and the Faiths We Never Knew* (New York: Oxford University Press, 2004), pp. 52–55. For details I am indebted to James A. Robinson, "Introduction," *The Nag Hammadi Library in English*, 4th rev. ed. (Leiden: Brill, 1996).

5. This information—about the skeleton—is not generally found in the published reports; I rely here on a private conversation that I had at the Scriptorium Conference, Hereford, England, with Bastiaan van Elderen (May 1998), who was the head of the archaeological team later responsible for exploring the site near Nag Hammadi.

6. See the authoritative account in Robinson, "Introduction," *Nag Hammadi Library in English*. Among the many, many studies of these writings, probably the most popular and influential has been Elaine Pagels, *The Gnostic Gospels* (New York: Random House, 1979).

7. For a translation of the letter, see Bart D. Ehrman and Andrew S. Jacobs, *Christianity in Late Antiquity 300–450 C.E.: A Reader* (New York: Oxford University Press, 2004) pp. 422–27.

Chapter Three

1.   See, for example, the collection in my book *Lost Scriptures: Books That Did Not Make It into the New Testament* (New York: Oxford University Press, 2004).

2.   Much of my discussion here is taken from my book *Lost Christianities: The Battles for Scripture and the Faiths We Never Knew* (New York: Oxford University Press, 2004), pp. 204–5.

3.   Much of this treatment is drawn from *Lost Christianities*, pp. 18–20.

4.   I have taken much of the following discussion from *Lost Christianities*, pp. 185–87.

5.   Translations of the Coptic Apocalypse of Peter are those of Birger Pearson, in *Nag Hammadi Codex VII*, ed. Birger Pearson (Leiden: Brill, 1996).

6.   I have taken much of this discussion from *Lost Christianities*, pp. 55–64.

7.   I am following the translation of Thomas Lambdin, found in *The Nag Hammadi Library in English*, 4th rev. ed., ed. James A. Robinson (Leiden: Brill, 1996).

8.   See Bart D. Ehrman, *The New Testament: A Historical Introduction to the Early Christian Writings*, 3rd ed. (New York: Oxford University Press, 2003), chap. 24.

9.   Compare the words of the first-century Jewish philosopher Philo: "For progress is indeed nothing else than the giving up of the female gender by changing into the male, since the female gender is material, passive, corporeal, and sense-perceptible, while the male is active, rational, incorporeal and more akin to mind and thought" (*Questions in Exodus*, 1.8). See further Dale B. Martin, *The Corinthian Body* (New Haven: Yale University Press, 1995), p. 33.

Chapter Four

1.   Some Jews, including Jesus, accepted other books as sacred as well—for example, the writings of the prophets and the Psalms.

2.   For a fuller discussion of the formation of the Christian canon of the New Testament, see Bart D. Ehrman, *Lost Christianities: The*

Battles for Scripture and the Faiths We Never Knew (New York: Oxford University Press, 2004), chap. 11.

3. See especially the Sermon on the Mount, Matthew 5–7.
4. See the discussion in Bart D. Ehrman, *The New Testament: A Historical Introduction to the Early Christian Writings*, 3rd ed. (New York: Oxford University Press, 2004), chap. 23.
5. For a fuller discussion of these disputes, see my book *Lost Christianities*, chap. 11.
6. For a full discussion of Marcion and his views, see *Lost Christianities*, chap. 5.
7. Irenaeus, *Against Heresies*, 3.11.7.
8. I have taken some of the following discussion from *Lost Christianities*, pp. 240–44.
9. Translation by Bruce M. Metzger, *The Canon of the New Testament: Its Origin, Development, and Significance* (Oxford: Clarendon Press, 1987), p. 305.
10. Eusebius is famously confusing, or confused, in the way he delineates the categories of (potentially) sacred books in this discussion. See Metzger, *Canon*, pp. 201–7.
11. Eusebius, *Life of Constantine*, 4.36. See Bruce M. Metzger and Bart D. Ehrman, *The Text of the New Testament: Its Transmission, Corruption, and Restoration*, 4th ed. (New York: Oxford University Press, 2004).

Chapter Five

1. For a fuller discussion of this, and all our other non-canonical sources, see Bart D. Ehrman, *Jesus: Apocalyptic Prophet of the New Millennium* (New York: Oxford University Press, 1999), chap. 4.
2. I give a fuller discussion in the work mentioned in the preceding note.
3. William V. Harris, *Ancient Literacy* (Cambridge, MA: Harvard University Press, 1989).
4. For Jewish literacy in the first century, see Catherine Hezser, *Jewish Literacy in Roman Palestine* (Tübingen : Mohr Siebeck, 2001).
5. For a fuller discussion, see Ehrman, *Jesus: Apocalyptic Prophet*, chap. 3.

6. Born of a woman (Gal 4:4), had twelve followers (1 Cor. 15:5) and several brothers (1 Cor. 9:5), one of whom was named James (Gal. 1:19), ministered to Jews (Rom. 15:8), instituted the Lord's Supper (1 Cor. 11:22–24), was handed over to the authorities (1 Cor. 11:22), and was crucified (1 Cor. 2:2).

7. This is true even of John 21:24, where the author refers to an eyewitness, "the one who testifies to these things," but speaks of him as someone other than himself. Notice what he says next: "and we know his [the eyewitness's] testimony is true." He is not claiming to be the eyewitness himself, but rather an author who is reporting what the eyewitness said.

8. For further information on these sources, and evidence of their existence, see Bart D. Ehrman, *The New Testament: A Historical Introduction to the Early Christian Writings*, 3rd ed. (New York: Oxford University Press, 2004), chap. 6.

9. See Ehrman, *The New Testament: A Historical Introduction*, chap. 10.

10. See Ehrman, *Jesus: Apocalyptic Prophet*, chap. 2.

Chapter Six

1. For a further explanation and justification of these criteria, see Bart D. Ehrman, *Jesus: Apocalyptic Prophet of the New Millennium* (New York: Oxford University Press, 1999), chap. 6.

2. For a more in-depth analysis, see Ehrman, *Jesus: Apocalyptic Prophet*, chaps. 8–11.

3. All of these claims have been made by scholars (and nonscholars) studying the historical Jesus. See my book *Jesus: Apocalyptic Prophet*, pp. 21–22.

Chapter Seven

1. Michael Baigent, Richard Leigh, and Henry Lincoln, *Holy Blood, Holy Grail* (New York: Delta, 1982).

2. Of the hundreds of professional New Testament scholars whom I personally know—people who study these texts for a living, and who are trained in the ancient languages necessary to do

so—there is not a single one, to my knowledge, who finds the claims of the book to be historically credible.

3. There is an enormous literature on women in early Christianity and its immediate environs. One of the most accessible is Ross Kraemer, *Her Share of the Blessings: Women's Religions Among Pagans, Jews, and Christians in the Greco-Roman World* (New York: Oxford University Press, 1992). See also the essays in Ross Kraemer and Mary Rose D'Angelo, *Women and Christian Origins* (New York: Oxford University Press, 1999).

4. Much of this is drawn from my treatment in *The New Testament: A Historical Introduction to the Early Christian Writings*, 3rd ed. (New York: Oxford University Press, 2004), chap. 24.

5. The most compelling and influential treatment has been that of Elizabeth Schüssler Fiorenza, *In Memory of Her: A Feminist Theological Reconstruction of Christian Origins* (New York: Crossroad, 1983).

6. Most notably William E. Phipps, *Was Jesus Married: The Distortion of Sexuality in the Christian Tradition* (Lanham, MD: University Press of America, 1986).

7. See the article on the Essenes by John Collins in the *Anchor Bible Dictionary*, ed. David Noel Freedman (New York: Doubleday, 1992), vol. 2, pp. 619–26.

Chapter Eight

1. Much of the following discussion is taken from my book *The New Testament: A Historical Introduction to the Early Christian Writings*, 3rd ed. (New York: Oxford University Press, 2004), chap. 24.

2. For a fuller discussion, see Bart D. Ehrman, *Lost Christianities: The Battles for Scripture and the Faiths We Never Knew* (New York: Oxford University Press, 2003), chap. 2. A recent translation of the tales can be found in Bart D. Ehrman, *Lost Scriptures: Books That Did Not Make It into the New Testament* (New York: Oxford University Press, 2003), pp. 113–21.

3. For the evidence, see Bart D. Ehrman, *The New Testament: A Historical Introduction to the Early Christian Writings*, 3rd ed. (New York: Oxford University Press, 2003), chap. 23.

4. Some readers will note that the verses in 1 Timothy sound strikingly similar to those found in a letter that Paul almost certainly

wrote, 1 Corinthians. There are reasons for thinking, however, that Paul did not actually write 1 Cor. 14:34–35, that these verses were added to his letter by a later scribe, based on his knowledge of 1 Tim. 2:11–15. See Ehrman, *New Testament: A Historical Introduction*, p. 402.

5. For fuller discussion, see Bart D. Ehrman, *Jesus: Apocalyptic Prophet of the New Millennium* (New York: Oxford University Press, 1999), pp. 16–17, and the bibliography cited there.

6. Translation of S. Thelwall, in the *Ante-Nicene Christian Library*, eds. Alexander Roberts and James Donaldson, vol. 11 (Edinburgh, T. & T. Clark, 1869), pp. 304–5.

7. A standard survey of Gnostic thought and its sources is Kurt Rudolph, *Gnosis: The Nature and History of Gnosticism*, trans. and ed. R. M. Wilson (San Francisco: Harper & Row, 1984); for a briefer discussion, see Ehrman, *Lost Christianities*, chap. 6.

8. For the following I am dependent on my comments in *Lost Scriptures*, p. 35.

9. For a translation, see that of George MacRae and R. McL. Wilson, in *The Nag Hammadi Library in English*, ed. James A. Robinson, pp. 524–27.

10. Here I rely on my comments in *Lost Scriptures*, p. 38.

11. For a translation, see that of Wesley W. Isenberg, in James A. Robinson, *Nag Hammadi Library in English*, 4th rev. ed. (Leiden: Brill, 1996), pp. 139–60.

12. See the range of opinions found in the collection of essays edited by Karen King, *Images of the Feminine in Gnosticism*, 2nd ed. (Harrisburg, PA: Trinity Press International, 2000).

13. See my discussion in *Lost Christianities*, pp. 198–201.

14. See my discussion in *Lost Christianities*, pp. 198–201.

Index

The Passion of the Christ (film),
xvi, 187
patriarchy of early Christianity,
4, 24, 171–72, 179, 183, 184
Patripassianism ("the Father
suffers"), 21
Paul, Acts of, 90
Paul, Epistles of: authorship,
170–71; canonization, 86, 89;
on Jesus' marital status, 153.
See also specific epistles
Paul (apostle): apocalypticism of,
157, 168; on divinity/mortal-
ity of Jesus, 15–16; on gender
issues, 181; on Jesus' life and
ministry, 109; as missionary,
166; quoting Jesus, 78–79;
recognition of gender differences, 180; view on women in
early church, 166–69, 171;
writings, 77–78, 88
Pentateuch, 76–77
Persecution, Great, 8
persecution of Christians, 7–8, 11
pessimism in apocalypticism, 33
Peter, Apocalypse of, 86, 87, 90
Peter, Coptic Apocalypse of, 56–
59
Peter, Epistles of: canonization,
89; date of documentation,
78, 79; disputed status, 89;
proscription of, 87
Peter, Gospel of, 53–56; discussion of Jesus, 108–9; on Jesus'
female followers, 149; on
Jesus' marital status, 153; on
Mary Magdalene, 159–60;
proscription of, 81–83, 88, 90

Peter (apostle): illiteracy, 107;
Jesus' appearance to, 55; on
Mary Magdalene, 68, 176;
role in early church, 165
Petronius, 54
Pharisees, 32, 150
Phibionites, 182–83
Philemon, 86
Philip, Gospel of, 177–79; on
Jesus' divinity/humanity, 44;
on Jesus' marital status, 153;
on Jesus' relationship with
Mary Magdalene, 108, 155,
159; on Mary Magdalene,
142, 143–44
Philip (disciple), 39, 166
Philippians, Epistle to: canonization of, 86; on divinity of
Jesus, 16; women addressed
by Paul, 167
Philo of Alexandria: discussion
of Jesus, 105; on Essenes,
155; on gender, 193n. 9
Pilate, Pontius: condemnation of
Jesus, 53; in historical
sources, 105, 106; resurrection of Jesus, 55
Pliny, 104–5, 156
polytheism: in early Christianity,
80, 174; in pagan communities, 5–6
Priory of Sion: descendants of
Jesus protected by, 141;
feminine emphasis, 24, 163–
64; in *Holy Blood, Holy Grail*,
142; on Mary Magdalene's
pregnancy, 143; Purist
Documents, 99